ON

MILL

Susan Leigh Anderson
University of Connecticut

Wadsworth
Thomson Learning™

Australia • Canada • Mexico • Singapore • Spain
United Kingdom • United States

Printed in the United States of America
1 2 3 4 5 6 7 03 02 01 00 99

For permission to use material from this text, contact us:
Web: http://www.thomsonrights.com
Fax: 1-800-730-2215
Phone: 1-800-730-2214

For more information, contact:
Wadsworth/Thomson Learning
10 Davis Drive
Belmont, CA 94002-3098
USA
http://www.wadsworth.com

ISBN: 0-534-57600-1

Contents

Preface

Chapter 1.   Mill's Life and the Evolution of his Views   1
Study Questions   31

Chapter 2.   Jeremy Bentham's "Hedonistic Calculus"   32
Study Questions   43

Chapter 3.   *Utilitarianism*   44
Study Questions   61

Chapter 4.   *On Liberty*   62
Study Questions   81

Chapter 5.   Final Assessment   82
Study Questions   89

Selected Bibliography   90

Preface

Eugene August asserts, in his book *John Stuart Mill, A Mind At Large*, that:

> Mill was the last great "Renaissance mind" of Western thought, imperially taking all knowledge for his province. He was also the first great interdisciplinary mind of the modern world, forging links among the various fields of learning to which he contributed so brilliantly. To a world beset by multiplicity of knowledge and narrow specialisms, Mill remains the grand instructive example of intellectual integration.[1]

In a brief introduction to Mill's philosophy, it would be impossible to do justice to all the work he did, to all the topics which he discussed in his writings. I shall not attempt to do this. Instead, I will concentrate on three of his most famous works: his *Autobiography, Utilitarianism* and *On Liberty*. From the first book we learn about his life, the development of his thought, and also something about the rest of his writings. In the other two books, which are undoubtedly his most widely read philosophical works, we see Mill apparently being pulled in opposite directions. The great battle that was being waged in the nineteenth century,[2] and still is being waged today, between the philosophies of Individualism and Collectivism, was being fought within his heart and mind.

Individualism is the view that the individual is the most important entity, that society exists in order to benefit individuals, not the other way around. Individuals should have the right to live their lives as they please, as long as they allow others to do the same. *Collectivism*, on the other hand, is the view that individuals are subservient to society. Individuals should be required to act for the benefit of society as a

---

[1] Eugene August, *John Stuart Mill, A Mind at Large*, Charles Scribner's Sons, New York, 1975, p. 5.

[2] Some of the clearest expressions, and strongest defenses, of Individualism and Collectivism were given by philosophers in that century. Consider the individualists Kierkegaard and Nietzsche, and the collectivists Hegel, Marx and Engels.

whole.[1] *On Liberty* appears, to many, to be the classic defense of Individualism; while *Utilitarianism* is certainly an argument for a collectivist philosophy. Can the two be reconciled? That is the main focus of this book.

I shall discuss Mill's *Utilitarianism* before *On Liberty*, even though they were published in the reverse order, for three reasons: (1) Mill's utilitarian philosophy predated the ideas which he expressed in *On Liberty*. (2) Mill attempts to justify his views in *On Liberty* using the philosophy of Utilitarianism, so one needs to know something about Utilitarianism to fully understand *On Liberty*. (3) Mill's particular version of Hedonistic Act Utilitarianism is based upon the ideas of Jeremy Bentham, with revisions motivated by a desire to correct the deficiencies in Bentham's work. I, therefore, feel it is important to have a chapter on the philosophy of Jeremy Bentham, with Mill's reaction to that philosophy. It seems appropriate to place that chapter between the chapter on Mill's life and the chapter on *Utilitarianism*, since Bentham was one of the three most important people in Mill's life.

The other two important people in Mill's life were his father and the love of his life and eventual wife, Harriet Taylor. Harriet once said to Mill, "you would be the most remarkable man of your age if you had no other claim to be so than your perfect impartiality and your fixed love of justice."[2] Few would question Mill's impartiality; but many would be surprised that he, as a utilitarian, could be described as a champion of justice. I shall try to explain, in Chapter Three, how Mill's "fixed love of justice" fits into his overall philosophy.

I am sorry not to have been able to say more about Mill's other works. I have tried to somewhat correct this deficiency by briefly describing the contents of his other major works in the opening chapter. In this way, readers may discover other works of Mill's which it might interest them to read.

I would like to thank William and David Alpert for their help and dedicate this book to my students, past and present, who have put up with my repeatedly claiming that the Individualism versus Collectivism debate is the central issue in Ethics and Politics.

---

[1] For a fuller discussion of these positions see my "Natural Rights and the Individualism versus Collectivism Debate," *The Journal of Value Inquiry*, Vol. 29, 1995, pp. 307-16.

[2] Hayek, F. A., *John Stuart Mill and Harriet Taylor*, Routledge and Kegan Paul, London, 1951, p. 114.

1

Mill's Life and the Evolution of his Views

John Stuart Mill was born in London on May 20th, 1806, the eldest son of James and Harriet Burrow Mill. James Mill (1773-1836) — philosopher, historian, economist and psychologist — was the most influential person in Mill's life during his formative years. It is, therefore, appropriate to begin the story of John Stuart Mill's life with some background on his father.

James Mill was the son of a humble Scottish country shoemaker. But his proud mother, who had known better days, was determined that her first-born son should be brought up as a gentleman. While his younger sister and brother were required to work in the shop, house and field, James was not permitted to do any manual work and devoted his time instead entirely to his studies. With the help of the local minister and Sir John and Lady Jane Stuart of Fettercairn, who were impressed with the young man, James was able to attend Montrose Academy and then sent to study for the ministry at the University of Edinburgh. Lady Jane was in charge of a fund which financed the training of poor young men for the Church.

James Mill
(From a drawing by Perugini)

At the age of seventeen, James was hired to tutor Sir John and Lady Jane's only daughter, Wilhelmina, who was then fourteen. He taught her for four years, at Edinburgh during the school year, where the Stuarts spent their winters, and at Fettercairn during the summers. He fell in love with her; but having an "iron will," he was able to control his feelings. We do not know what Wilhelmina thought of her handsome, young, blue-eyed tutor, but she ended up marrying the son of the banker Sir William Forbes and later inspired a romantic passion in Sir Walter Scott. Some biographers maintain that Wilhelmina was the love of James Mill's life.

While at Edinburgh, James discovered Plato. He would later pass on his tremendous admiration for this philosopher to his son. James also read a number of skeptics — including Rousseau, Voltaire and Hume — with the result that he ended up not following the profession that he was trained for, "having satisfied himself that he could not believe the doctrines of [the Scottish Church] or any other Church."[1]

After Edinburgh, James supported himself by tutoring for a few more years in Scotland. While working for a Mr. Burnet of Elrick, he was apparently dismissed from the table by a motion of the thumb and,

---

[1] John Stuart Mill, *Autobiography*, The Library of Liberal Arts, New York, 1957, p. 4.

as a result, walked out of the house never to return. To react to a "person of quality" in this way was unheard of behavior for the son of a village shoemaker.[1]

In 1802, at the age of twenty-nine, James Mill left Scotland for London in the company of Sir John Stuart. He soon had a small income from writing for periodicals and editing, and in 1805 he married pretty Harriet Burrow who was about ten years younger than he was and the eldest daughter of a widow who ran a private lunatic asylum. They moved into a small house in Pentonville which was owned by Mrs. Burrow. John Stuart Mill, named after the squire of Fettercairn, was born the next year. The vivacious Harriet was concerned with appearances and hoping for a more sociable life. She soon resented the family's modest circumstances; and the impatient, sarcastic James, who perhaps missed the responsive intelligence he had found in Wilhelmina, began treating his wife more and more like a *hausfrau*. Although they produced nine children, there was very little affection in the relationship between James and his wife. Perhaps John picked up on his father's dismissal of his mother as not being very important. Her existence is entirely ignored in his *Autobiography*.

James Mill was an extremely disciplined and hard working man. In the year of his eldest son's birth he began to write a history of British India. He expected the project to take three years and believed it would make his name. It ended up taking ten years to write his *History of India*, which became the standard work on the subject. It was published, in three volumes, in 1817, and led to an appointment at the East India Company in 1819. There James Mill prepared drafts of dispatches to India, which finally gave him and his family economic security.

Meanwhile, James spent a considerable part of almost every day on the education of his children, especially his eldest son. James had unlimited faith in the power of education, and he particularly stressed the early training of character. Perseverance, temperance and self-restraint were three of his most important virtues. He was extremely suspicious of strong emotion, perhaps because of his own romantic failures: his unrequited love for Wilhelmina and the momentary passion which led to his unhappy marriage. As his son said of him:

---

[1] See Ruth Borchard, *John Stuart Mill, the Man*, Watts Publishing Company, London, pp. 4-5.

For passionate emotions of all sorts, and for everything which has been said or written in exhaltation of them, he professed the greatest contempt. He regarded them as a form of madness.[1]

Unfortunately, James Mill's control over his feelings affected his relationship with his children, at least the older ones. It is heartbreaking to read John's impartial assessment of his father on this score, reading between the lines to see how much it must have hurt John to have received so little affection from the father he tried so hard to please:

> The element which was chiefly deficient in his moral relation to his children was that of tenderness. I do not believe that this deficiency lay in his own nature. I believe him to have had much more feeling that he habitually showed, and much greater capacities of feeling than were ever developed. He resembled most Englishmen in being ashamed of the signs of feeling, and by the absence of demonstration, starving the feelings themselves. If we consider further that he was in the trying position of sole teacher, and add to this that his temper was constitutionally irritable, it is impossible not to feel true pity for a father who did, and strove to do, so much for his children, who would have so valued their affection, yet who must have been constantly feeling that fear of him was drying it up at its source. This was no longer the case later in life, and with his younger children. They loved him tenderly; and if I cannot say so much of myself, I was always loyally devoted to him.[2]

James Mill's older children were too much afraid of him to love him, but it is clear that John admired his father greatly. He lived for the rare moments when his father seemed to approve of him.

In 1808 James Mill met Jeremy Bentham, the patriarch of the English Utilitarians, who was then sixty years old. (More will be said about Bentham in the next chapter.) He soon became Bentham's "lieutenant," and Bentham did what he could to help the Mill family through the early period of financial difficulty. In 1810 he installed the Mills in a cottage, where John Milton had once lived, on the grounds of

---

[1] *Autobiography*, p. 33.

[2] *Ibid.*, pp. 34-5.

4

his own house at No. 2 Queen Square Place; but they found it too dank to stay very long and soon moved to Newington Green. Four years later Bentham tried again. He leased a house, close to his own, at No. 1 Queen Square Place, and then sublet it to the Mills for a nominal fee. This was John's home from his eighth to his twenty-fourth years. During the summers, Bentham took the entire family to his country retreats, first to Barrow Green House in the Surrey Hills, and later to Ford Abbey, a wonderful country estate where ornamental Tudor work alternated with Inigo Jones additions. John particularly enjoyed its spacious rooms and the opportunity to take long walks, exploring the rolling hills of rural England. He also liked listening to Bentham playing the Abbey organ.

John later wrote of the bond that united his father with the much older Bentham:

> [My] father was the earliest Englishman of any great mark, who thoroughly understood, and in the main adopted, Bentham's general views of ethics, government and law; and this was a natural foundation for sympathy between them, and made them familiar companions in a period of Bentham's life during which he admitted much fewer visitors than was the case subsequently.[1]

Although not the original thinker that Bentham was, James Mill's personality drew a small circle of active reformers around them both. This group became known as the "philosophical radicals" for advocating democracy and complete freedom of discussion. These men were the avant-garde of their time, just as the Fabians were seventy-five years later. During his lifetime, James Mill wrote numerous articles which applied Benthamite principles to such subjects as government, education, freedom of the press, colonies, jurisprudence and prisons. He also wrote several books, the most notable of which, besides his *History of India*, were *Elements of Political Economy* (1821) and *Analysis of the Phenomena of the Human Mind* (1829).

Despite all these achievements, James Mill's greatest creation was his own son. As James Mill confided in Bentham, young John Stuart Mill had been selected to be "a successor worthy of both of us." In preparation for filling this role, John was given perhaps the most

---

[1] *Autobiography*, p. 36.

rigorous and ambitious education that anyone has ever received, an education later described in great detail in Mill's *Autobiography*. So important was John's education to James Mill that he wrote to Bentham, in 1812 during an illness, that:

> If I were to die any time before this poor boy is a man, one of the things that would pinch me most sorely, would be the being obliged to leave his mind unmade to the degree of excellence of which I hope to make it.[1]

At three years of age, John was given lessons in Greek and soon began reading in that language, beginning with *Æsop's Fables*. When he was eight, he began studying Latin and added works in that language. His days were taken up with studying and then teaching what he had learned to his younger siblings, which he hated doing, although he admitted later that it helped him to learn how to explain things to others. He had no toys or children's books, except for a few gifts given to him by relatives or acquaintances, most notably a treasured *Robinson Crusoe*. He had no friends to play with — his father limited his contact with other young boys because "he was earnestly bent upon [his] escaping not only the ordinary corrupting influence which boys exercise over boys, but the contagion of vulgar modes of thought and feeling"[2] — and his only exercise consisted of taking long walks with his father, reciting and discussing what he'd learned that day.

By his twelfth year, in addition to having read the Greek classics and even Aristotle's *Rhetoric*, John had learned algebra, geometry and differential calculus. He had also written a number of "histories." Also, despite his father's caring little for English poetry and so John's being asked to read very little of it, he was required to write verses in addition to prose, which he disliked. His father explained that "some things could be expressed better and more forcibly in verse" than prose and "people in general attached more value to verse than it deserved, and the power of writing it was, on this account, worth acquiring."[3] John also enjoyed reading about science; but he was not given a chance to do any experiments, which he would have enjoyed.

At age twelve he began studying logic, beginning with the Latin treatises on scholastic logic. John claimed that the "first intellectual

---

[1] Alexander Bain, *James Mill,* London, 1882, p. 119.

[2] *Autobiography*, p. 24.

[3] *Ibid.*, p. 11.

operation in which I arrived at any proficiency, was dissecting a bad argument, and finding in what part the fallacy lay." Later he asserted that the study of logic was a good activity for young philosophy students. He thought they "may become capable of disentangling the intricacies of confused and self-contradictory thought, before their own thinking faculties are much advanced" and that the study of logic would "form exact thinkers, who attach a precise meaning to words and propositions."[1] Demonstrating his firm belief in utilitarian principles, James Mill emphasized the *utility* of the study of logic:

> It was his invariable practice, whatever studies he exacted from me, to make me as far as possible understand and feel the utility of them; and this he deemed particularly fitting in the case of the syllogistic logic, the usefulness of which had been impugned by so many writers of authority.[2]

John continued reading in Latin and Greek, particularly the orations and also, at this time, he began reading the most important dialogues of Plato. About Plato's influence on both father and son, John said:

> There is no author to whom my father thought himself more indebted for his own mental culture, than Plato....I can bear similar testimony in regard to myself.[3]

At the age of thirteen, James Mill gave John a complete course on political economy, giving him lectures which John had to clearly, precisely and completely summarize, and then having him read Adam Smith as well as a book which had just been published by James' good friend David Ricardo, *Principles of Political Economy and Taxation*.

James Mill seemed to have expected too much from the young boy, for even though John had praise for his excellent education, maintaining that "in the main his method was right, and it succeeded," he complained that his father "was often, and much beyond reason, provoked by my failures in cases where success could not have been expected...."[4] Still, John was not very critical of his father on this

---

[1] *Autobiography*, pp. 14-15.

[2] *Ibid.*, pp. 13-14.

[3] *Ibid.*, pp. 15-16.

[4] *Ibid.*, p. 20.

account, since he was convinced that "a pupil from whom nothing is ever demanded which he cannot do, never does all he can."[1] John later expressed concern about the opposite tendency "in modern teaching, to render as much as possible of what the young are required to learn, easy and interesting to them," fearing that it may end up "training up a race of men who will be incapable of doing anything which is disagreeable to them."[2]

At fourteen, John's formal "lessons" concluded, when he was invited to spend a year in France with Jeremy Bentham's brother, Sir Samuel, and his family. From this time on, although his studies continued under his father's general direction, there were no longer formal lessons.

Mill concluded, in his *Autobiography*, that as a result of the formal instruction which he received from his father, he started life "with an advantage of a quarter of a century over my contemporaries." However, John did not feel superior to others because of this:

> If I thought anything about myself, it was that I was rather backward in my studies, since I always found myself so, in comparison with what my father expected from me.[3]

John Stuart Mill believed that "any boy or girl of average capacity and healthy physical constitution" could have accomplished what he had, since he modestly believed he was "rather below than above par" in natural talent. What he thought was best about the education he received was that he was not "crammed with mere facts, and with the opinions or phrases of other people," using this as a substitution for forming opinions of one's own. Instead:

> My father never permitted anything which I learnt to degenerate into a mere exercise of memory. He strove to make the understanding not only go along with every step of the teaching, but, if possible, precede it. Anything which could be found out by thinking I never was told, until I had exhausted my efforts to find it out for myself.[4]

---

[1] *Autobiography*, p. 22.
[2] *Ibid.*, p. 35.
[3] *Ibid.*, p. 23.
[4] *Ibid.*, p. 22.

One controversial aspect of John's upbringing was that he was raised without any religious beliefs. Not only did his father find "it impossible to believe that a world so full of evil was the work of an Author combining infinite power with perfect goodness and righteousness," but he looked upon religion "as the greatest enemy of morality." He complained that religion held up as the ideal of perfect goodness a Being who created Hell, that is, a Being:

> who would create the human race with the infallible foreknowledge, and therefore with the intention, that the great majority of them were to be consigned to horrible and everlasting torment.[1]

Not only is this abhorrent, according to James Mill, which believers, with their "slovenliness of thought," do not seem to realize; but as long as people look to religion for morality, "morality continues to be a matter of blind tradition, with no consistent principle, nor even any consistent feeling, to guide it."

Mill states, in his *Autobiography*, that as a result of his anti-religious upbringing:

> I am thus one of the very few examples, in this country, of one who has, not thrown off religious belief, but never had it; I grew up in a negative state with regard to it.[2]

The opinions on the subject of religion which James passed on to his son could have been a problem for young John, since others would have found these sentiments to be offensive. It was only his "limited intercourse with strangers, especially such as were likely to speak to [him] on religion" which prevented him from "being placed in the alternative of avowal [of atheism] or hypocrisy." John Stuart Mill continued, throughout his life, to be disturbed by the automatic connection most people make between the rejection of religion and "bad qualities of either mind or heart." As a result of this prejudice, atheists tend to keep silent about their beliefs. Mill suspected that:

> The world would be astonished if it knew how great a proportion of its brightest ornaments — of those most

[1] *Autobiography*, p. 28.
[2] *Ibid.,*, p. 29.

9

distinguished even in popular estimation for wisdom and virtue — are complete skeptics in religion....[1]

The evening before John left for his trip to France in 1820-21, James prepared John for the reaction he would likely receive to his unusual upbringing. He told him that, upon making the acquaintance of new people, they would soon discover that he had been taught many things which people of his age did not typically know and that "many persons would be disposed to talk to you of this, and to compliment you upon it." But, John recorded in his *Autobiography*, James ended his conversation with his son by saying that:

> whatever I knew more than others, could not be ascribed to any merit in me, but to the very unusual advantage which had fallen to my lot, of having a father who was able to teach me, and willing to give the necessary trouble and time; that it was no matter of praise to me, if I knew more than those who had not had a similar advantage, but the deepest disgrace to me if I did not.[2]

John's year in France was a happy one. He enjoyed his first taste of freedom, "breath[ing] for a whole year, the free and genial atmosphere of Continental life."[3] He spent most of the time continuing his studies, writing detailed accounts of the work he did to his father; but the Benthams insisted that he also learn to fence and ride, neither of which he enjoyed, and to dance, which to his great surprise, he loved. John also learned the French language and read classic French literature, and he spent much time in the company of the Benthams' oldest son George who introduced him to the joys of plant collecting during their long walks together. This became a lifelong hobby for John.

The Benthams did not stay in one place during this year. John traveled with them from Pompignan to the Pyrenees, where he discovered a passion for the mountains, and then to an estate near Montpellier. John took university courses at the Faculté des Sciences during their six months at Montpellier, and he made a friend in a French student of his own age.

---

[1] *Autobiography*, p. 30.
[2] *Ibid.*, p. 24.
[3] *Ibid.*, p. 38.

John was particularly impressed with the competent and dignified Lady Bentham, the daughter of a celebrated chemist, who was the undisputed head of the Bentham household. To see the roles reversed from what they were in his own home showed him the potential to be found in women. He was also impressed by "the frank sociability and amiability of French personal intercourse" which he observed as being in marked contrast to the English habit of "acting as if everybody else (with few, or no exceptions) was either an enemy or a bore." [1]

John returned to England to find his father just finishing his *Elements of Political Economy*. John was asked to summarize each paragraph, an exercise which Jeremy Bentham did with all of his writings, "to enable the writer more easily to judge of, and improve, the order of the ideas, and the general character of the exposition." Soon after, he began studying the French Revolution which, he recorded in his *Autobiography*, "took an immense hold of my feelings." He also "read Roman law" during the winter of 1821-2 with John Austin who "had made Bentham's best ideas his own, and added much to them from other sources and from his own mind."

At the beginning of these studies, James gave John, whose entire education had prepared him for the acceptance of the "principle of utility," his first direct taste of Jeremy Bentham's ideas when he had him read Dumont's three volume exposition and translation of some of Bentham's published and unpublished works, the *Traité de Législation Civile et Pénale*. The reading of this work he later said was "an epoch in my life, one of the turning points in my mental history." In his *Autobiography*, John wrote of the tremendous impact reading the *Traité* had on his life:

> What...impressed me was the chapter in which Bentham passed judgment on the common modes of reasoning in morals and legislation, deduced from phrases like "law of nature," "right reason," "the moral sense," "natural rectitude," and the like, and characterized them as dogmatism in disguise, imposing its sentiments on others....It had not struck me before, that Bentham's principles put an end to all this. The feeling rushed upon me, that all previous moralists were superseded, and that here indeed was the commencement of a new era in thought. This impression was strengthened by the manner in which Bentham put into scientific form the

---

[1] *Autobiography*, p. 39.

application of the happiness principle to the morality of actions....As I proceeded further, there seemed to be added to this intellectual clearness, the most inspiring prospects of practical improvements in human affairs....When I laid down the last volume of the *Traité*, I had become a different being....I now had opinions; a creed, a doctrine, a philosophy; in one of the best senses of the word, a religion.....And I had a grand conception laid before me of changes to be effected in the condition of mankind through that doctrine....[T]he vista of improvement which [Bentham] did open was sufficiently large and brilliant to light up my life, as well as to give definite shape to my aspirations.[1]

John continued to read what he could of Bentham's work, in addition to advanced work in "analytic psychology," under his father's direction. He read Locke, Helvetius, Hartley, Berkeley, Hume, Reid and others, as well as a book, published under the pseudonym of Richard Beauchamp, titled *Analysis of the Influence of Natural Religion on the Temporal Happiness of Mankind* which impressed John because it was critical of the usefulness of religious belief.

From the summer of 1822 on, when he wrote his first argumentative essay, John "began to carry on [his] intellectual cultivation by writing still more than by reading."[2] At this point he could only manage to compose a "dry argument." He also conversed more with learned friends of his father's and began to feel "a man among men," rather than "a pupil under teachers."

In the winter of 1822-3, John formed a society composed of young men who accepted Utility "as their standard in ethics and politics." They met every two weeks for a period of three and a half years. John decided to call the group the "Utilitarian Society" and "the term ['Utilitarian'] made its way into the language from this humble source." John acknowledged that he'd gotten the term from a novel he'd read, Galt's *Annals of the Parish*.

In May of 1823, James Mill obtained a position for John at the East India Company in the office of the Examiner of India Correspondence, initially working immediately under his father as a clerk and ending up as Examiner, two years before the closing of the East India Company forced his retirement in 1858. James chose this

---

[1] *Autobiography*, pp. 42-4.

[2] *Ibid.*, p. 46.

occupation for his son because he thought it would allow him time to think and write. He fully expected his son to make his mark not only on England, but upon the world. Mill came, in time, to realize that it would have been impossible for him to make his living as a writer of the kind of books he wanted to write; and other occupations to which he was attracted, such as running for Parliament, would have left him little time to think and write. He found his work to be "sufficiently intellectual not to be a distasteful drudgery, without being such as to cause any strain upon the mental powers."[1] It also gave him practical experience in public affairs which he thought was of much value to him as a theoretician:

> I became practically conversant with the difficulties of moving bodies of men, the necessities of compromise, the art of sacrificing the non-essential to preserve the essential. I learnt how to obtain the best I could, when I could not obtain everything...[2]

The main drawback of his job for him was being confined to London, with only a month of vacation time allowed each year. His trip to France had given him a taste for country living and travel.

The year he began working for the East India Company, John began writing for newspapers, starting with letters to the editor. Some of these letters, supporting the publication of all opinions on religion, appeared in the *Morning Chronicle*, written under a pseudonym. The *Morning Chronicle*, edited by John Black, increasingly became "a vehicle of the opinions of the Utilitarian radicals." So did the *Westminster Review*, established by Bentham in 1823, which "made the so-called Bentham school in philosophy and politics fill a greater place in the public mind than it had held before, or has ever again held."[3] John was the most frequent contributor, eventually having thirteen articles published in the *Review*.

The "Utilitarian radicals" did not entirely agree with one another on their views. John Stuart Mill commented, in his *Autobiography*, on a difference of opinion between his father and himself and his friends:

---

[1] *Autobiography*, p. 54.

[2] *Ibid.*, p. 55.

[3] *Ibid.*, p. 65.

[H]e maintains that women may consistently with good government, be excluded from the suffrage, because their interest is the same with that of men. From this doctrine, I, and all those who formed my chosen associates, most positively dissented.[1]

John was convinced that "every reason which exists for giving the suffrage to anybody, demands that it should not be withheld from women." He was pleased that Bentham agreed with him on this important matter.

At this time of his life, John maintained that he had become a Benthamite "reasoning machine." He had inherited his father's and Bentham's suspicion of feelings, the undervaluing of poetry — according to Bentham, "all poetry is misrepresentation" — and imagination in general.

About 1825, Bentham asked John to edit his five-volume work, which had been written much earlier, *Rationale of Judicial Evidence*. It took him about a year of his leisure time, but John thought it well worth the time, since it contained "very fully developed, a great proportion of all [Bentham's] best thoughts" and also "it gave a great start to my powers of composition."

In addition to his editing assignment and writing for the *Westminster Review*, John continued his studies. He learned German and he formed a study group which took up political economy, then syllogistic logic and finally analytic psychology. The discussions of logic led to his forming the idea of eventually writing a book on logic. The study group, Mill believed, was very important to his development:

> I have always dated from these conversations my own real inauguration as an original and independent thinker. It was also through them that I acquired, or very much strengthened, a mental habit to which I attribute all that I have ever done, or shall ever do, in speculation; that of never accepting half-solutions of difficulties as complete; never abandoning a puzzle, but again and again returning to it until it was cleared up; never allowing obscure corners of a subject to remain unexplored, because they did not appear important; never

---

[1] *Autobiography*, p. 67.

thinking that I perfectly understood any part of a subject until I understood the whole.[1]

From 1825 to 1829, John did some public speaking. A debate with the Owenites led to the formation of a debating society, which took up so much of John's time that he was relieved when the *Westminster Review* faltered. His last article, in the spring of 1828, concerned the French Revolution which continued to interest him. He had the intention, at this time, of some day writing a history of the French Revolution, but it never came to pass.

In the autumn of 1826, when he was just twenty years old, John suffered a mental breakdown. Since first reading Bentham in the winter of 1821, he had known what he wanted to do with his life: "to be a reformer of the world."[2] His own happiness was entirely bound up in that goal. But then one day, in a mood when he found himself "unsusceptible to enjoyment or pleasurable excitement":

> In this frame of mind it occurred to me to put the question directly to myself: "Suppose that all your objects in life were realized; that all the changes in institutions and opinions which you are looking forward to, could be completely effected at this very instant: would this be a great joy and happiness to you?" And an irrepressible self-consciousness distinctly answered, "No!" At this my heart sank within me: the whole foundation on which my life was constructed fell down....I seemed to have nothing left to live for.[3]

Months went by and John's depression only deepened. He had no one to whom he felt he could turn, no one to whom he felt really close, which was part of the problem. It was clear that his upbringing, which had turned him into a veritable thinking machine, had harmed him by neglecting an important aspect of the human psyche: the emotions. "I now saw," he said later in his *Autobiography*, "that the habit of analysis has a tendency to wear away the feelings."

To show how overly analytical his thinking had become, Mill gave, as an example, a concern he had that we would soon run out of new musical compositions to give people pleasure:

---

[1] *Autobiography*, pp. 79-80.

[2] *Ibid.*, p. 86.

[3] *Ibid.*, p. 87.

[T]he pleasure of music...fades with familiarity, and requires either to be revived by intermittence, or fed by continual novelty. And it is very characteristic both of my then state, and of the general tone of my mind at this period of my life, that I was seriously tormented by the thought of the exhaustibility of musical combinations. The octave consists only of five tones and two semi-tones, which can be put together in only a limited number of ways, of which but a small proportion are beautiful; most of these, it seemed to me must have been already discovered....[1]

Mill managed to continue with his "usual occupations," doing them "mechanically, by the mere force of habit;" but he didn't think he could go on living in this way for very long. Fortunately, after about six months, "a small ray of light broke in upon [his] gloom":

I was reading, accidentally, Marmontel's "Mémoires," and came to the passage which relates his father's death, the distressed position of the family, and the sudden inspiration by which he, then a mere boy, felt and made them feel that he would be everything to them — would supply the place of all they had lost. A vivid conception of the scene and its feelings came over me, and I was moved to tears. From this moment my burthen grew lighter. The oppression of the thought that all feeling was dead within me, was gone. I was no longer hopeless: I was not a stock or a stone. I had still, it seemed, some of the material out of which all worth of character, and all capacity for happiness, are made.[2]

After this experience, he began to find enjoyment again in nature, books, conversations and public affairs; and, although there were some relapses, he was never again as miserable as he had been. Mill learned two things from what he had gone through: (1) To be happy, you must focus on something else:

Those only are happy (I thought) who have their minds fixed on some object other than their own happiness....Aiming thus at something else, they find happiness by the way. The

---

[1] *Autobiography*, p. 94.
[2] *Ibid.*, p. 91.

enjoyments of life (such was now my theory) are sufficient to make it a pleasant thing, when they are taken *en passant*, without being made a principal object. Once make them so, and they are immediately felt to be insufficient. They will not bear a scrutinizing examination. Ask yourself whether you are happy, and you cease to be so. The only chance is to treat, not happiness, but some end external to it, as the purpose of life.[1]

Mill did not give up his conviction that "happiness is the test of all rules of conduct, and the end of life," but he had discovered the *hedonist paradox*, that the only way to find happiness is not to think about it.

(2) Mill also learned from his ordeal that "the cultivation of the feelings" is as important as the cultivation of other capacities: "The maintenance of a due balance among the faculties, now seemed to me of primary importance."[2] To put this into practice in his own life, Mill began reading poetry to supplement his long-standing love of music. After first trying to read Byron, but finding that "the poet's state of mind was too like [his] own" depressed state, he discovered Wordsworth, whose poetry "proved to be the precise thing for [his] mental wants at that particular juncture."[3] Wordsworth's love of natural scenery, particularly the mountains, revived feelings already latent in Mill, and he found that the appreciation of the beauty of nature could coexist in a mind which had been scientifically trained:

> The intensest feeling of the beauty of a cloud lighted by the setting sun, is no hindrance to my knowing that the cloud is vapour of water, subject to all the laws of vapours in a state of suspension; and I am just as likely to allow for, and act on, these physical laws whenever there is occasion to do so, as if I had been incapable of perceiving any distinction between beauty and ugliness.[4]

It was not only in his realization of the importance of the emotions and a newfound interest in poetry that Mill started to break away, ideologically, from his father. By participating in the Debating Society,

[1] *Autobiography*, p. 92.
[2] *Ibid.*, p. 93.
[3] *Ibid.*, p. 95.
[4] *Ibid.*, p. 98.

which he quit in 1829, Mill had come to realize, while trying to defend Bentham's and his father's views, some of the difficulties with their simplistic theory of government. He now saw that "identity of interest between the governing body and community at large is not...the only thing on which good government depends...."[1] By now Mill felt "at a great distance" from his father in many respects, but he believed that "no good,...only pain to both of us" would come from discussing their differences.

Looking for new input, Mill became interested in the St. Simonian School in France, particularly the views of Auguste Comte. What struck him about this school, which was at that time only in its earliest stages of speculation, besides "proclaiming the perfect equality of men and women," was the belief in "the natural order of human progress" and "their division of all history into organic periods and critical periods." From this, Mill later wrote,

> I obtained a clearer conception than ever before of the peculiarities of an era of transition in opinion, and ceased to mistake the moral and intellectual characteristics of such an era, for the normal attributes of humanity. I looked forward...to a future which shall unite the best qualities of the critical with the best qualities of the organic periods; unchecked liberty of thought, unbounded freedom of individual action in all modes not hurtful to others; but also, convictions as to what is right and wrong, useful and pernicious, deeply engraven on the feelings by early education and general unanimity of sentiment....[2]

Mill began to realize that his mission was to assist England, and perhaps the rest of the world as well, in making the transition from a critical period into a new organic period.

Despite his hopeful prognosis and a renewed sense of purpose in his life, Mill had occasional relapses of depression. During one of these, he fretted over Determinism, or what was then called the doctrine of "Philosophical Necessity." He was concerned that "[his] character and that of all others had been formed for us by agencies beyond our control, and was wholly out of our own power."[3]

---

[1] *Autobiography*, p. 102.
[2] *Ibid.*, p. 107.
[3] *Ibid.*, p. 109.

Gradually, however, he realized that Determinism did not have to be viewed as something negative. Indeed, this doctrine allowed for the possibility that our will could causally affect our behavior, which would give us control over what happened to us, rather than deny us that control. The fear of Determinism stems from confusing it with Fatalism, the view that, no matter what we want or do, such-and-such will happen. This confusion has arisen due to the ambiguity in the word "necessity," which Mill thought should be avoided:

> I perceived, that the word Necessity, as a name for the doctrine of Cause and Effect applied to human action, carried with it a misleading association; and that this association was the operative force in the depressing and paralysing influence which I had experienced. I saw that though our character is formed by circumstances, our own desires can do much to shape those circumstances; and what is really enspiriting and ennobling in the doctrine of free-will, is the conviction that we have real power over the formation of our own character; that our will, by influencing some of our circumstances, can modify our future habits or capabilities of willing. All this was entirely consistent with the doctrine of circumstances, or rather, was that doctrine itself, properly understood. From that time I drew in my own mind, a clear distinction between the doctrine of circumstances, and Fatalism; discarding altogether the misleading word Necessity. The theory, which I now for the first time rightly apprehended, ceased altogether to be discouraging....[1]

This insight of Mill's, an early attempt at formulating the now popular position known as Soft-Determinism or Compatibilism — the position which accepts both Determinism, that every event has a cause, and free will/moral responsibility — he eventually published in a chapter on "Liberty and Necessity" in the concluding book of his *System of Logic*.

In addition to contributing to several newspapers, Mill wrote five essays — later published as *Essays on Some Unsettled Questions of Political Economy* — in 1830-31. Also in 1831, Mill attempted to state some of his new views on government, inspired in part by the French Revolution, in a series of articles titled *The Spirit of the Age*. Mill thought "the predominance of the aristocratic classes, the noble and the

---

[1] *Autobiography*, p. 109.

rich, in the English Constitution, an evil worth any struggle to get rid of."[1] It bothered him that "riches, and the signs of riches, were almost the only things really respected, and the life of the people was mainly devoted to the pursuit of them."[2] He also hoped to convince those in power that "they had more to fear from the poor when uneducated, than when educated."[3] The uneducated poor, for instance, might be impressed with the socialist views of the Owenites and St. Simonians, but through education be convinced that there are advantages to allowing private property. His series impressed Thomas Carlyle enough — he initially thought that "here is a new Mystic" — for him to come out of seclusion in Scotland to meet Mill. Mill's characteristic modesty, or honesty, lead him to write in his *Autobiography*: "I felt that [Carlyle] was a poet, and that I was not; he was a man of intuition, which I was not."[4]

Mill returned again to questions of logic, puzzling over "the great paradox of the discovery of new truths by general reasoning" since he believed that "all reasoning is resolvable into syllogisms, and that in every syllogism the conclusion is actually contained and implied in the premises."[5] He continued to read widely in logic, finding some inspiration in the work of Dugald Stewart. Finally, Mill began to put his own thoughts down on paper.

Meanwhile, in 1830, when he was twenty-five years old, Mill had met a woman who, he said, was by this time in the process of becoming "the honour and chief blessing of my existence, as well as the source of a great part of all that I attempted to do, or hope to effect hereafter, for human improvement."[6] This woman was Harriet Hardy Taylor who, when they first met, was the twenty-three year old wife of John Taylor, a wholesale druggist, and the mother of two children. Generally known as "a beauty and a wit, with an air of natural distinction," she had married her older husband — an "honourable man, of liberal opinions and good education, but without the intellectual or artistic tastes which would have made him a companion for her,"[7] according to Mill — at a very young age. Although she had been raised to think that a

---

[1] *Autobiography*, p. 110.

[2] *Ibid.*

[3] *Ibid.*, p. 111.

[4] *Ibid.*, p. 113.

[5] *Ibid.*, p. 116.

[6] *Ibid.*, p. 119.

[7] *Ibid.*, p. 120.

Harriet Taylor
(ca. 1834)

respectable marriage and family was all that a woman should aspire to, Harriet had come to discover the drawbacks of her marriage. The sexual part had come as an unpleasant shock to her and she found the role of "a businessman's household ornament"[1] to be unfullfilling. As a woman, she was "shut out by the social disabilities of women from any adequate exercise of her highest faculties in action on the world without,"[2] but Mill had incredibly high praise for her abilities and her character. Not all agreed with Mill's assessment of Harriet Taylor. While Mill "worshipped Mrs. Taylor as an embodiment of all that was excellent in human nature,"[3] others saw her as "only a spoiled, would be bluestocking."[4] In any case, Harriet Taylor was not only the great love of John Stuart Mill's life, but she also became Mill's collaborator on many of his greatest works. He claimed that he "acquired more from her teaching, than from all other sources taken together"[5] and that "all

---

[1] August, *Op. Cit.*, p. 48.

[2] *Ibid.*

[3] Leslie Stephen, *The English Utilitarians*, Vol. III, Peter Smith Publishing Company, New York, p. 44.

[4] August, *Op. Cit.*, p. 47

[5] *Autobiography*, p. 122.

my published writings were as much [her] work as mine; her share in them constantly increasing as years advanced."[1]

Harriet Taylor could neither part with her husband, nor forgo Mill's company. The three settled into "a thoroughly respectable version of a *ménage à trois*, with John Taylor conveniently dining out a lot and John Mill calling during specified hours."[2] John and Harriet's relationship was Platonic and her marriage apparently also became so after Helen Taylor's birth in 1831. Mill's family and friends disapproved of his relationship with Harriet, causing Mill to break with many of them as Harriet became the most important person in his life.

In 1834 Mill published abstracts of several of Plato's dialogues, together with introductory remarks, which he had written several years earlier. Also in the same year, he consented to become the editor of a new review, initially called the *London Review*, which was intended to take the place of the *Westminster Review*. This occupied much of his spare time between 1834 and 1840.

Mill's father's health declined during 1835 and he died in June of 1836 of "pulmonary consumption." While Mill acknowledged all that his father had done for him, he admitted that:

> Deprived of my father's aid, I was also exempted from the restraints and reticences by which that aid had been purchased. I did not feel that there was any other radical writer or politician to whom I was bound to defer....I resolved henceforth to give full scope to my own opinions and modes of thought....[3]

After a five year break, Mill resumed work on his *System of Logic* in 1837. He finished it in 1840; and the following year, as he did with each of his books, he rewrote it. During the rewriting of his *System of Logic*, Mill was able to incorporate material from Comte as well as present his ideas in the form of a rebuttal to Whewell's's *Philosophy of the Inductive Sciences* which had just come out. Mill's *System of Logic* was published in 1843. It was an immediate success, being adopted as a text first at Oxford and then later at Cambridge, but also read by many outside the universities. *System of Logic* was Mill's first attempt at a comprehensive statement of his empiricist and utilitarian views and an

---

[1] *Autobiography*, p. 157.
[2] August, *Op. Cit.*, p. 48.
[3] *Autobiography*, pp. 132-3.

attack on "intuitionism." With this book Mill hoped to demonstrate that an empiricist position could lead to knowledge, guide social planning and political action, and not just lead to skepticism as Hume had argued.

Mill's *Logic* was divided into six books. In the first two books Mill presented an empiricist theory of deductive inference, giving his solution to the paradox which had once troubled him of how we seem to be able to discover new truths through syllogistic reasoning, since the conclusion is contained in the premises. He claimed that, although the conclusion of a syllogism does not contain more than was in the premises, those premises which are generalizations are in fact *empirical* generalizations. Consider, for example, the syllogism "All men are mortal, Smith is a man, therefore Smith is mortal." "All men are mortal" is an empirical generalization, according to Mill, arising from inductive reasoning, and this explains why we feel that we have learned something in drawing the conclusion that "Smith is mortal." Even mathematical knowledge is no exception to this, according to Mill. Although the conclusions of mathematical reasoning follow necessarily from the premises, the premises themselves, the axioms, are in fact empirical generalizations.

In Book III of the *Logic*, Mill discussed the grounds and methods of inductive reasoning. According to Mill, there are four basic inductive methods: the Method of Agreement, the Method of Difference, the Method of Residues, and the Method of Concomitant Variation. He also added a method which is a combination of the first two, calling it the Joint Method of Agreement and Difference. Book IV, titled "Of Operations Subsidiary to Induction," contains chapters on observation and description, abstraction, naming, and classification. In Book V, Mill discussed fallacies; and in the final book, Book VI, Mill attempted to extend his empirical methods to psychology, sociology and morality. He argued for the possibility of a science of human behavior, although he admitted that we will at best probably only discover tendencies towards acting in such-and-such a way, because of the enormous number of factors which determine human behavior.

Harriet Taylor, who suffered from ill health, spent much of each year in the country with her young daughter, only occasionally visiting her husband in London. Mill saw her in both places and their relationship strengthened. In their discussions, they found themselves leaning more towards a socialist economy, while "repudiat[ing] with the greatest energy that tyranny of society over the individual which most socialist systems are supposed to involve:"[1]

> The social problem of the future we considered to be, how to unite the greatest individual liberty of action, with a common ownership in the raw material of the globe, and an equal participation of all in the benefits of combined labour.[2]

"Education, habit, and the cultivation of the sentiments" is what they thought was needed to change human beings from egoists into beings who are interested in the common good. They believed it could come about one day, but that the social conditions of their day tended to reinforce selfishness:

> Interest in the common good is at present so weak a motive in the generality, not because it can never be otherwise, but because the mind is not accustomed to dwell on it as it dwells from morning till night on things which lead only to personal advantage....The deep-rooted selfishness which forms the general character of the existing state of society is *so* deeply rooted, only because the whole course of existing institutions tends to foster it....[3]

This view was increasingly incorporated into the *Principles of Political Economy*, completed in 1847, as it went though several editions. Also included was Mill's new belief that a representative form of democracy was better than the pure form. The reading of Alexis de Tocqueville's *Democracy in America* had a hand in convincing him of this. As with his *Logic*, Mill's *Principles of Political Economy* was an immediate success, which he attributed to the fact that it was an applied work, not just theory, and that it treated the subject of political economy as a branch of the larger topic of social philosophy.

For quite a while after this, Mill confined himself to writing in periodicals on subjects of public interest and writing essays for eventual publication. He was not very encouraged by public events. He thought there were two reasons why there was no progress: (1) There would be no real improvements in the "lot of mankind" "until a great

---

[1] *Autobiography*, p. 148.

[2] *Ibid.*, p. 149.

[3] *Ibid.*

change takes place in the fundamental constitution of their modes of thought." (2) In the absence of any real convictions, like those which religion can provide, there isn't enough faith in anything to provide real guidance:

> When the philosophic minds of the world can no longer believe its religion, or can only believe it with modifications amounting to an essential change in its character, a transitional period commences, of weak convictions, paralysed intellects, and growing laxity of principle, which cannot terminate until a renovation has been effected in the basis of their belief leading to the elevation of some faith, whether religious or merely human, which they can really believe....[1]

Harriet's husband died in July, 1849 and, after a suitable period of mourning, Harriet and John married in April of 1851. Two weeks before the wedding, Mill signed a document renouncing the "odious powers" English law at that time gave husbands over wives and promising Harriet as much freedom to act and dispose of her property, including a half-share in Mill's books, as if the marriage did not take place. They had but seven and a half married years together; and although Mill claimed in his *Autobiography* that marriage added to "the partnership of thought feeling, and writing which had long existed, a partnership of our entire existence,"[2] it is doubtful that their relationship was ever sexually consummated. Harriet had been an invalid for years and now Mill's own health began to deteriorate. He had his first attack of "the family disease," tuberculosis, which forced him to take a leave of absence from the India House for more than six months, during which time a journey to Italy and Greece helped him to regain his health.

In 1854 Mill began working on a short essay which, the next year, he decided to turn into the book eventually published under the title *On Liberty*. None of his other books was "so carefully composed" or "so sedulously corrected" as this one. In addition to his usual practice of writing it twice, he and Harriet continued to look at it, from time to time, "weighing and criticizing every sentence."

In 1856, Mill was promoted to the rank of Examiner of India Correspondence, second in rank only to the Secretary of the East India

---

[1] *Autobiography*, p. 153.
[2] *Ibid.*, p. 154.

Company. He held this position for only two years and then Parliament decided to dissolve the company, despite Mill's fight to prevent it. The closing of the company turned out to be personally beneficial for him, however, since his newfound leisure afforded him more time for his writing and he was granted liberal retirement benefits.

Mill planned to do the final revision of *On Liberty* in France during the winter of 1858-9, the first after his retirement; but tragedy struck when Harriet died of "a sudden attack of pulmonary congestion" in Avignon. Mill bought a cottage as close as possible to the place where Harriet was buried and there he and Helen Taylor, Harriet's daughter, decided to live for most of each year. Harriet's memory became, for Mill, "a religion"; and he dedicated the rest of his life to pursuing their common goals.

After suffering his "irreparable loss," Mill returned to the task of finishing *On Liberty*, the book which he said "was more directly and literally [his and Harriet's] joint production than anything else which bears my name" and which he correctly anticipated "is likely to survive longer than anything else" he wrote. He wanted to "consecrate it to [Harriet's] memory." *On Liberty* was published in 1859 and had "an electrifying effect on the ardent men and women of the younger generation."[1] John Morely wrote of it:

> I do not know whether then or at any other time so short a book ever instantly produced so wide and so important an effect on contemporary thought as did Mill's *On Liberty* in that day of intellectual and social fermentation.[2]

Following *On Liberty*, the political circumstances of the time inspired Mill to complete and publish a pamphlet which he'd started a number of years before, *Thoughts on Parliamentary Reform*. One of his ideas for reform was to give more votes to those with "proved superiority of education," an idea which "found favor with nobody." Mill next published a selection, which he and Harriet had chosen together, of his minor writings, under the heading *Dissertations and Discussions*. After this, Mill turned to completing two works for publication, *Considerations on Representative Government* and *Utilitarianism*. The latter work was first published in *Fraser's Magazine* and afterwards printed as a book.

---

[1] Borchard, *Op. Cit.*, p. 128.
[2] Quoted in Borchand, *Op. Cit.*, p. 128.

Mill also at this time wrote *The Subjection of Women*, at Helen Taylor's suggestion, but he delayed publishing it until "the time when it should seem likely to be most useful." In this work — said to be "the only major work of feminist theory written by a man who is generally considered a great theorist within the western political tradition"[1] — Mill argued that every Victorian wife was, by law, a slave. Even if most women, in addition to all men, were satisfied with the arrangement, it is not consistent with "utility in the largest sense, grounded on the permanent interests of man as a progressive being," which he had argued, in *On Liberty*, is "the ultimate appeal on all ethical questions." Against the view that we can see, from historical observation, that patriarchy is natural, Mill argued that we cannot say what is natural for women, or men for that matter, until we observe them living in circumstances where neither is under the control of the other.

Instead of the existing patriarchal arrangement, Mill advocated a "principle of perfect equality" in the relationship between the sexes, where there is "no power or privilege on the one side, nor disability on the other." He argued that everyone would benefit from living within households based on equality and friendship, even the children who learn their first lessons about what is just in the home.

The American Civil War had begun by the time Mill finished *The Subjection of Women*, and Mill believed that it "was destined to be a turning point, for good or evil, of the course of human affairs."[2] He wrote an essay for *Fraser's Magazine*, titled "The Contest in America," which appeared in January, 1862.

For the next two years Mill worked on *An Examination of Sir William Hamilton's Philosophy*. Hamilton was the leading defender of the philosophy of intuitionism and much admired. Mill felt if reform was ever to be possible, it was extremely important to refute "a philosophy which is addicted to holding up favourite doctrines as intuitive truths, and deems intuition to be the voice of Nature and of God, speaking with authority higher than that of our reason."[3]

Mill next decided to "undertake the task of sifting what is good from what is bad in M. Comte's speculations." Since Mill was responsible, more than anyone else, for making Comte known to

---

[1] Susan M. Okin, editor, *The Subjection of Women*, by John Stuart Mill, Hackett Publishing Company, Indianapolis, 1988.

[2] *Autobiography*, p. 171.

[3] *Ibid.*, p. 175.

John Stuart Mill
(ca. 1865)

English audiences, he thought he had a responsibility to do this. He wrote two essays, published first in the *Westminster Review*, and then as a book titled *Auguste Comte and Positivism*.

In 1865, Mill received a proposal which, if he acted on it, would mark a great change in the purely literary life into which he had settled. He was asked to stand for election to become a member of the House of Commons. It was not the first such offer, but he hadn't been able to consider earlier offers, when he was employed at the East India House, since a conflict of interest might have arisen.

Mill had unusual views about candidates running for office:

> Now it was, and is, my fixed conviction, that a candidate ought not to incur one farthing of expense for undertaking a public duty....that the expense, or any part of it, should fall on the candidate [who is then forced to raise funds], is fundamentally wrong; because it amounts to buying his seat....and (a consideration of the greatest importance) the cost of elections, when borne by the candidates, deprives the nation of the services, as members of Parliament, of all who cannot or will not afford to incur a heavy expense.[1]

---

[1] *Autobiography*, pp. 179-80.

Mill would only consider running, if he did not have to raise funds or use his own money. He, further, stipulated that if elected he would not spend time on "local interests;" and, in answer to questions posed to him, he told them frankly that he supported women's suffrage — which is said to have started the women's suffrage movement in England — and that he would answer no questions about his views on religion. His terms were accepted and he thought that his honesty was much appreciated:

> My frankness...evidently did me far more good than my answers, whatever they might be, did harm. Among the proofs I received of this, one is too remarkable not to be recorded. In the pamphlet, "Thoughts on Parliamentary Reform," I had said, rather bluntly, that the working classes, though differing from those of some other countries, in being ashamed of lying, are yet generally liars. This passage some opponent got printed in a placard, which was handed to me at a meeting, chiefly composed of the working classes, and I was asked whether I had written and published it. I at once answered "I did." Scarcely were these two words out of my mouth, when vehement applause resounded through the whole meeting. It was evident that the working people were so accustomed to expect equivocation and evasion from those who sought their suffrages,...they concluded at once that this was a person whom they could trust.[1]

Mill was elected and helped to pass the Reform Bill. There was little time for writing; he only had time during the recesses, but he did publish a few things during this period, including a pamphlet on Ireland and an essay on Plato. In 1868, the Parliament was dissolved and Mill was not reelected. He was relieved to return to a private life lived mostly in France, near his wife's grave, with occasional visits to London.

The Subjection of Women was published in 1869, during a period of feminist activism following Mill's championing of women's rights while he was a member of Parliament. The work was highly controversial at the time. The conservative Victorian moralist James Fitzjames Stephen called it "a work from which I dissent from the first

---

[1] *Autobiography*, pp. 181-2.

sentence to the last;"[1] but Elizabeth Cady Stanton's reaction was to say, "I lay the book down with a peace and joy I never felt before."[2]

Mill died at Avignon, on May 8th, 1873, after a sudden attack, "having three days before walked fifteen miles on a botanical excursion."[3] His last words were: "You know that I have done my work."[4] He was laid to rest beside Harriet, in the small St. Véran Cemetery outside the ancient walled city of Avignon. Mill's *Autobiography*, which he had begun in 1853 and added to over the years, was published a few months after his death.

Summing up his life, Leslie Stephen said:

> [Since] he was singularly candid, fair in argument, most willing to recognize merits in others, and a staunch enemy of oppression in every form, we may say that Mill possessed in an almost unsurpassable degree the virtues particularly appropriate to a philosopher....[H]e was from his youth upwards devoted to the spread of principles which he held to be essential to human happiness. No philanthropist...could labour more energetically and unremittingly for the good of mankind....Whatever his limitations, he brought the whole energy of a singularly clear, comprehensive, and candid intellect to bear upon the greatest problems of his time...[5]

[1] James Fitzjames Stephen, *Liberty, Equality, Fraternity*, in Andrew Pyle, Editor, *The Subjection of Women, Contemporary Responses to John Stuart Mill*, Thoemmes Press, Bristol, England, 1995, p. 243.
[2] Alma Lutz, *Created Equal: A Biography of Elizabeth Cady Stanton*, John Day Company, New York, 1940, p. 171.
[3] Stephen, *Op. Cit.*, p. 68.
[4] Borchard, *Op. Cit.*, p. 148.
[5] Stephen, *Op. Cit.*, pp. 69-74.

Study Questions

1. Discuss the advantages and disadvantages of Mill's unusual upbringing and education.

2. What were the two things Mill learned from his mental breakdown?

3. Why do people fear Determinism and why, according to Mill, should they not? Do you agree with him?

4. Have things changed much since Mill complained that, in his day, "riches, and the signs of riches, were almost the only things really respected, and the life of the people was mainly devoted to the pursuit of them"?

5. Do you agree with Mill that it is possible to change human beings from egoists into beings who are interested in the common good? Do you, too, believe that the "deep-rooted selfishness which forms the general character of the existing state of society is *so* deeply rooted, only because the whole course of existing institutions tends to foster it"?

6. Is Mill right that when there isn't something which people *really* believe in — "the elevation of some faith, whether religious or merely human" — there will be a period "of weak convictions, paralysed intellects, and general laxity of principle"? Is this a problem with our own age?

7. What is your reaction to Mill's conditions for his running for political office?

2

Jeremy Bentham's "Hedonistic Calculus"

Jeremy Bentham was born in Houndsditch, London in 1748. His father, Clerk of the Scriveners' Company and a prosperous man, sent Jeremy to Westminster School in 1755. He entered Queen's College, Oxford in 1760 at the age of twelve and graduated when he was just fifteen, in 1763. Bentham then immediately entered Lincoln's Inn to study law. He passed the bar exam in 1767, when he was nineteen; but he never practiced law. Bentham was very dissatisfied with what he had witnessed in the courts as a student and with theories of law put forth by men such as Blackstone. Instead of practicing law, Bentham undertook the task of working out a system of jurisprudence and codifying and reforming civil and penal law. He spent his life advocating a clear, rational and humane legal system.

In 1768, Bentham stumbled upon the basis of that system when, upon returning to Oxford to vote at a University parliamentary election, he happened to go into a circulating library and found a copy of Joseph Priestly's new pamphlet, *Essay on Government*. In it he found the phrase "the greatest happiness of the greatest number." Of this discovery, he said:

It was by that pamphlet and this phrase in it that my principles on the subject of morality, public and private, were determined. It was from that pamphlet and that page of it that I drew the phrase, the words and the import of which have been so widely diffused over the civilized world.[1]

Although he wrote thousands of pages during his lifetime, the only major work which Bentham published himself was the *Introduction to the Principles of Morals and Legislation* (Oxford, 1789). His enormous reputation on the Continent was the result of French translations of various papers given by Bentham to his early disciple Étienne Dumont. Bentham left unfinished his mammoth *Constitutional Code*, which he had worked on for years; but he did publish numerous pamphlets which exposed abuses and urged reform. His idea for a model prison was sanctioned by an Act of Parliament in 1794, but in the end nothing came of it. It did, however, convince him of the desirability of a democracy since he was sure that the only reason why such a good idea was not acted upon was that Parliament did not represent the people and did not have their real interests at heart.[2]

Bentham died in 1832, leaving his body for dissection — the first person known to have done so — to the Webb Street School of Anatomy. He then requested that his embalmed body, topped with a waxen copy of his head and dressed in his usual clothes, be displayed at University College, London, where it can still be seen to this day.

To understand what had so impressed Mill when he first read the work of Jeremy Bentham, and also how Mill tried to improve upon Bentham's utilitarian philosophy, it is important that we examine just what Bentham had to say. Let us, therefore, consider the main points of the first four chapters of Bentham's greatest work, *An Introduction to the Principles of Morals and Legislation.*

In Chapter One, "Of the Principle of Utility," Bentham states that he accepts the view now known as Hedonism, that all and only pleasure (or happiness) is intrinsically good, and its opposite, pain (or unhappiness), is intrinsically bad. The desire to increase pleasure or happiness, and avoid pain or unhappiness, not only determines how we *do* act, but how we *ought to* act. This forms the basis of his "principle of utility," which he later called "the greatest happiness principle":

---

[1] See Mary Warnock's Introduction to *Utilitarianism and Other Writings*, New American Library, New York, 1974, p. 7.
[2] *Ibid.*, p. 8.

> By the principle of utility is meant that principle which approves or disproves of every action whatsoever, according to the tendency which it appears to have to augment or diminish the happiness of the party whose interest is in question; or, what is the same thing in other words, to promote or to oppose that happiness.[1]

Whose happiness and unhappiness should we consider? Bentham makes it clear that it is the entire "community," not just certain individuals. But what is the "community"?

> The community is a fictitious *body*, composed of the individual persons who are considered as constituting as it were its members. The interest of the community then is, what? — the sum of the interests of the several members who compose it.[2]

Having indicated whose interests are to be taken into account, Bentham is able to give what we would now consider to be a very imprecise statement of Hedonistic Act[3] Utilitarianism: "An action then may be said to be conformable to the principle of utility...when the tendency it has to augment the happiness of the community is greater than any it has to diminish it."[4] Compare this with the definition of Hedonistic Act Utilitarianism which I currently give my students: That act is right which, of all the alternative actions open to the agent, is likely to result in the greatest net pleasure (or happiness) or the least displeasure (or unhappiness), taking everyone affected by the action into account.

Despite the imprecision of Bentham's principle, we can see why Mill and others were so impressed with it. The reigning ethical principle of the day was Kant's Categorical Imperative: Act always in such a way that you could wish the maxim of your action (that is, the principle on which you are acting) to become universal law. This

---

[1] Jeremy Bentham, *An Introduction to the Principles of Morals and Legislation*, in Warnock, *Op. Cit.*, p. 34.

[2] *Ibid.*, p. 35.

[3] Act Utilitarianism, as opposed to Rule Utilitarianism, evaluates particular actions rather than general practices. This distinction was not made until the twentieth century.

[4] *An Introduction to the Principles of Morals and Legislation*, p. 35.

Jeremy Bentham
(Portrait by H. W. Pickersgill)

essentially amounts to maintaining that you should act in the way in which you would like to see everyone act. What if you are a sado-masochist? You would feel justified in torturing someone, because you would be quite happy having everyone act in this way. The problem with Kant's Categorical Imperative is that it is so subjective. Utilitarianism is an ethical theory designed to remove the subjectivity from ethical decision-making, by using the likely consequences of your actions, which at least in theory can be objectively determined, as the basis for ethical decision-making. It corrects for individual bias, by forcing the agent to take into account *everyone's* response to the action.

After having stated his principle, Bentham considers whether it is "susceptible of any direct proof" and his answer is: "it should seem not: for that which is used to prove everything else, cannot itself be proved."[1] Although his principle of utility is not capable of direct proof, Bentham does proceed to give, in the remainder of Chapter One and in Chapter Two, "Of Principle Adverse to that of Utility," a long, impressive indirect argument to support the principle of utility. The argument — a series of separation of cases arguments in which he reduces every other option for justifying an ethical decision to absurdity — begins by assuming that there are just two general

[1] *An Introduction to the Principles of Morals and Legislation*, p. 36.

positions: Either one decides how to act without using any principle, instead doing whatever one feels like doing, or else one uses a principle.

If the first, either one imposes one's own inclinations on everyone else, which he claims is "despotical, and hostile to all the rest of the human race," or else one allows that "every man's sentiment has the same privilege of being a standard to itself." He dismisses this individual form of Ethical Relativism as being "anarchical" and points out other undesirable consequences of accepting this view, that:

> whether even to the sane man, the same thing, which is right to-day, may not (without the least change in its nature) be wrong to-morrow? and whether the same thing is not right and wrong in the same place at the same time? and in either case, whether all argument is not at an end? and whether, when two men have said, "I like this," and "I don't like it," they can... have any thing more to say?[1]

Turning to the second branch of the argument, Bentham claims that there are just three possible principles, or types of principles, on which one may act: First, one may act on the principle of utility. Second, one may act on the principle which is the opposite of the principle of utility, which he labels the "principle of asceticism." Third, and finally, one could act on a principle which is "sometimes opposed to [the principle of utility] and sometimes not," which he calls a "principle of sympathy and antipathy."

Concerning the principle of asceticism, Bentham accuses its followers of inconsistency. He says there are two types of individuals who support the principle of asceticism, the principle "approving of actions in as far as they tend to diminish happiness; disapproving of them in as far as they tend to augment it": a set of "moralists" and a set of "religionists." The moralists hope to receive "honour and reputation at the hands of men" for sacrificing their own pleasure, but this amounts to the hope of receiving pleasure in the future. The religionists fear the punishment of God unless they sacrifice their own pleasure; but, since they are trying to avoid pain, they too are following the principle of utility. In any case, Bentham points out another fundamental inconsistency with the principle of asceticism:

---

[1] *An Introduction to the Principles of Morals and Legislation*, p. 39.

The principle of asceticism, however, with whatever warmth it may have been embraced by its partisans as a rule of private conduct, seems not to have been carried to any considerable length, when applied to the business of government. ...Whatever merit a man may have thought there would be in making himself miserable, no such notion seems ever to have occurred to any of them, that it may be a merit, much less a duty, to make others miserable....[1]

Bentham concludes that:

The principle of asceticism never was, nor ever can be, consistently pursued by any living creature. Let but one tenth part of the inhabitants of this earth pursue it consistently, and in a day's time they will have turned it into a hell.[2]

The third type of principle one could follow, a principle of sympathy and antipathy, Bentham maintains amounts to following no principle at all, "avoiding the obligation of appealing to any external standard," since this type of principle is described by Bentham as:

[a] principle which approves or disapproves of certain actions, not on account of their tending to augment the happiness, nor yet on account of their tending to diminish the happiness of the party whose interest is in question, but merely because a man finds himself disposed to approve or disapprove of them: holding up that approbation or disapprobation as a sufficient reason for itself....[3]

It would seem that Bentham has just *defined* this category in such a way that he will be able to dismiss it easily. He points out, however, that defenders of this sort of "principle" invariably end up appealing to something like a "moral sense," "common sense," the "understanding," "natural justice," or "God's will," to justify their intuition of what is the right thing to do, and that this is just a disguise for personal sentiment determining which actions are right.[4]

---

[1] *An Introduction to the Principles of Morals and Legislation*, pp. 42-3.
[2] *Ibid.*, pp. 44-5.
[3] *Ibid.*, pp. 46-7.
[4] As an example, Bentham has us consider using "God's pleasure" as a

What Bentham's extended argument comes down to is that either one appeals to an external, objective standard of right and wrong, and then only the principle of utility seems to him to be reasonable and able to be consistently followed, or else one relies on one's subjective intuition, which may or may not be disguised in the form of something external, but this amounts to not following a principle at all.

In Chapter Three, Bentham discusses the four "sanctions," or sources of pleasure and pain: the *physical*, the *political*, the *moral*, and the *religious*. The *physical* is obvious. Mill later summarized the purpose of the other three:

> Bentham's idea of the world is that of a collection of persons pursuing each his separate interest or pleasure, and the prevention of whom from jostling one another more than is unavoidable, may be attempted by hopes and fears derived from three sources — the law, religion, and public opinion. To these three powers, considered as binding human conduct, he gave the name *sanctions*: the *political* sanction, operating by the rewards and penalties of the law; the *religious* sanction, by those expected from the Ruler of the Universe; and the *popular*, which he characteristically calls also the *moral* sanction operating through the pains and pleasures arising from the favour or disfavour of our fellow-creatures.[1]

In Chapter Four, Bentham raises the important question of how one is to measure pleasure and pain. We are all certainly capable of doing the "moral arithmetic," performing the "hedonistic calculus" — that is, adding up all the pleasure units and all the pain units and subtracting the later from the former — but how do we get the original numbers? The easiest way would be to assign to each person who will be affected by the action a "+1" or "-1", depending upon whether the person is likely to be pleased or displeased by the action; but Bentham realizes that this is inadequate. One person may be mildly pleased for a short time, if the agent were to do the action, whereas another person's

---

guide for action: "But what is God's pleasure? God does not, he confessedly does not now, either speak or write to us. How then are we to know his pleasure? By observing what is our own pleasure, and pronouncing it to be his." (*Ibid.*, footnote, p. 56.)

[1] John Stuart Mill, "Bentham," originally published in the *London and Westminster Review*, August, 1838, in Warnock, *Op. Cit.*, pp. 102-3.

entire life could be ruined by that same action. To assign a "+1" and a "-1", respectively, to each of these effects, so that they cancel each other out, would not properly reflect the consequences of the action.

Bentham says that we must consider, not just whether each person is likely to be pleased or displeased by the action, but also the *intensity*, *duration*, degree of *certainty*, *propinquity*, *fecundity* ("the chance it has of being followed by sensations of the *same* kind") and *purity* ("the chance it has of *not* being followed by sensations of the *opposite* kind") of the pleasure or displeasure. To determine the consequences of an action, this has to be done for each person who is likely to be affected by the action. Then the moral arithmetic can be done to figure out which action is likely to result in the greatest net good units of pleasure, or the least displeasure if the choice is between alternatives which are each likely to cause only displeasure.

At this point the reader is probably thinking that this theory is too complicated to ever use. Bentham anticipates this objection:

> It is not to be expected that this process should be strictly pursued previously to every moral judgment, or to every legislative or judicial operation. It may, however, be always kept in view; and as near as the process actually pursued on these occasions approaches to it, so near will such process approach to the character of an exact one.[1]

In other words, do the best you can in the time allowed. There is a built-in limit to the amount of time you should spend calculating. You should never spend so much time calculating that, because you missed the opportunity of performing an action, your taking the extra time calculating is likely to result in less than the greatest net good consequences.

Seventeen years after the time when he found his "creed," his "religion," in the work of Jeremy Bentham, Mill attempted to give a balanced assessment of Bentham's philosophy,[2] considering what he had learned as a result of his own mental breakdown. Mill praised Bentham for being "the great *subversive*, or, in the language ·of continental philosophers, the great *critical* thinker of his age and country": "who, before Bentham...dared to speak disrespectfully, in express terms, of the British Constitution, or the English Law?"

---

[1] *An Introduction to the Principles of Morals and Legislation,* p. 66.
[2] "Bentham," *Op. Cit.*

Mill also admired Bentham's analytic method:

> Whenever he found a *phrase* used as an argument for or
> against anything, he insisted upon knowing what it meant;
> whether it applied to any standard, or gave intimation of any
> matter of fact relevant to the question; and if he could not find
> that it did either, he treated it as an attempt on the part of the
> disputant to impose his own individual sentiment on other
> people, without giving them a reason for it....He has thus, it is
> not too much to say, for the first time introduced precision of
> thought into moral and political philosophy. Instead of taking
> up their opinions by intuition...philosophers are now forced to
> understand one another, to break down the generality of their
> propositions, and join a precise issue in every dispute. This is
> nothing less than a revolution in philosophy.[1]

Using his method primarily on the Law, which was always Bentham's
real interest,[2] "he found the philosophy of law a chaos, he left it a
science," according to Mill. Bentham recognized that laws should be
viewed "in a practical light, as means to certain definite and precise
ends."

Mill basically agreed with Bentham's ultimate end: the greatest net
happiness, for the greatest number of people. Even though he grew to
have concerns about the details, Mill thought that Bentham was right in
seeing that only a *teleological* theory of ethics, that is a theory which
bases the rightness and wrongness of actions entirely upon the
consequences of the actions, was defensible:

> Whether happiness be or be not the end to which morality
> should be referred — that it be referred to an *end* of some sort,
> and not left in the dominion of vague feeling or inexplicable
> internal conviction, that it be made a matter of reason and
> calculation, and not merely of sentiment, is essential to the
> very idea of moral philosophy; is, in fact, what renders
> argument or discussion on moral questions possible. That the
> morality of actions depends on the consequences which they

---

[1] "Bentham," pp. 87-91.

[2] "His was an essentially practical mind. It was by practical abuses that
his mind was first turned to speculation...." (*Ibid.*, p. 82.)

tend to produce is the doctrine of rational persons of all schools....[1]

Although there was so much that he admired about Bentham, there were three respects in which Mill thought that Bentham's philosophy was too narrow.[2] First, in calculating the consequences of actions, he did not acknowledge some of "the deeper feelings of human nature,"[3] feelings which not only exist in human beings, according to Mill, but which should be valued more highly than others. Mill, as we shall see in the next chapter, wanted to introduce differences in *quality* between pleasures, whereas for Bentham "to say either that man should, or that he should not, take pleasure in one thing, displeasure in another, appeared to him as much an act of despotism in the moralist as in the political ruler."[4]

What sort of feelings, which Mill particularly valued, did he think Bentham ignored?

> Man is never recognized by him as being capable of pursuing spiritual perfection as an end; of desiring, for its own sake, the conformity of his own character to his standard of excellence, without hope of good or fear of evil from other source than his own inward consciousness....[5]

Mill believed that Bentham, in his concern primarily for the Law, focused entirely on the regulation of people's "outward actions," ignoring another crucial part of morality: "self-education; the training by the human being himself, of his affections and will."[6]

Second, Mill questioned Bentham's claiming that the goal of political action is that which leads to the greatest happiness of the

---

[1] "Bentham," p. 120.

[2] Mill forgave Bentham for his narrowness: "For our own part, we have a large tolerance for one-eyed men, provided their one eye is a penetrating one; if they saw more, they probably would not see so keenly, nor so eagerly pursue one course of inquiry." (*Ibid.*, p. 98.)

[3] "He saw...in man little but what the vulgarest eye can see....Knowing so little of human feelings, he knew still less of the influences by which those feelings are formed...." (*Ibid.*, p. 97.)

[4] *Ibid.*, p. 101.

[5] *Ibid.*, p. 100.

[6] *Ibid.*, p. 103.

greatest number (the majority) at a given moment in time: "Is it, we say, the proper condition of man, in all ages and nations, to be under the despotism of Public Opinion?"[1] Mill can understand the desire for majority rule, given that in his day:

> European reformers have been accustomed to see the numerical majority everywhere unjustly depressed, everywhere trampled upon, or at the best overlooked, by governments; nowhere possessing power enough to extort redress of their most positive grievances....[2]

However, Mill had serious concerns about majority rule:

> The numerical majority of any society whatever, must consist of persons all standing in the same social position, and having, in the main, the same pursuits... and to give to any one set of partialities, passions and prejudices, absolute power, without counter-balance from partialities, passions, and prejudices of a different sort, is...to make one narrow, mean type of human nature universal and perpetual, and to crush every influence which tends to the further improvement of man's intellectual and moral nature.[3]

The third criticism Mill had of Bentham was that he "treat[ed] the *moral* view of actions and characters, which is unquestionably the first and most important mode of looking at them, as if it were the sole one; whereas it is only one of three."[4] In addition to the moral aspect of actions, Mill thought there is also the *aesthetic* aspect (its "beauty") and the *sympathetic* aspect (its "loveableness"). Mill says, for example, that Brutus' action in sentencing his sons for conspiracy was *morally* right, "but there was nothing *loveable* in it." According to Mill, "sentimentality consists in setting the last two of the three above the first; the error of moralists in general, and of Bentham, is to sink the two latter entirely."[5]

---

[1] "Bentham," p. 114.

[2] *Ibid.*, p. 115.

[3] *Ibid.*, pp. 115-6.

[4] *Ibid.*, p. 121.

[5] *Ibid.*, p. 122.

Mill thought Bentham was wrong in, for instance, rejecting the importance of the idea of "*good* and *bad* taste" and in claiming that "all poetry is misrepresentation." According to Mill, Bentham's later writings, in which all his sentences have so many qualifications in them to make sure that each one could stand alone as being true, amounts to "a *reductio ad absurdum* of his objection to poetry." Better to have well-crafted overgeneralizations or partial truths, in which there is "a little more than the truth in one sentence, and [a] correct[ion] in the next," than, for the sake of precision, "stop nowhere short of unreadableness"!

Mill's overall assessment of Bentham was that:

> He was a man both of remarkable endowments for philosophy, and of remarkable deficiencies for it: fitted, beyond almost any man, for drawing from his premises, conclusions not only correct, but sufficiently precise and specific to be practical; but whose general conception of human nature and life, furnished him with an unusually slender stock of premises.[1]

Mill's task, as he saw it, was to enlarge the number of premises, while retaining Bentham's method and basic principle.

Study Questions

1. Summarize and evaluate Bentham's indirect argument in defense of his principle of utility.

2. Try to apply Bentham's principle of utility to an ethical dilemma you recently found yourself in. Can you see how the principle requires you to be objective in reaching a decision? Do you have any difficulties in trying to follow the principle? Do you agree with what the principle tells you to do?

3. What did Mill admire in Bentham and what criticisms did he have of Bentham's philosophy?

---

[1] "Bentham," p. 97.

3

Utilitarianism

In Chapter One of *Utilitarianism*, under "General Remarks," Mill states the aim of his book:

> I shall ... attempt to contribute something towards the understanding and appreciation of the Utilitarian or Happiness theory, and towards such proof as it is susceptible of.[1]

He hastens to add, agreeing with Bentham:

> It is evident that this cannot be proof in the ordinary and popular meaning of the term. Questions of ultimate ends are not amenable to direct proof.[2]

Mill maintains that the principle of utility "has had a large share in forming the moral doctrines even of those who most scornfully reject its authority."[3] He believes that those who reject the theory do so largely because they don't fully understand it.

---

[1] John Stuart Mill, *Utilitarianism*, in Warnock, New American Library, New York, 1974, p. 254.

[2] *Ibid.*

[3] *Ibid.* Mill thinks this is even true of Kant, the leading deontologist (someone who does not base the rightness and wrongness of actions on

Before turning to an explanation and defense of Utilitarianism, Mill gives two general principles which should guide us in developing an ethical theory. He says, first, that:

> All action is for the sake of some end, and rules of action, it seems natural to suppose, must take their whole character and colour from the end to which they are subservient.[1]

This principle reveals Mill's bias towards adopting the teleological approach to ethical theory — that is, basing the rightness and wrongness of actions on the consequences of those actions — which not all would accept. His second principle, on the other hand, is one which most action-based ethicists[2] would agree with:

> there ought either to be some one fundamental principle or law, at the root of all morality, or if there be several, there should be a determinate order of precedence among them; and the one principle, or the rule for deciding between the various principles when they conflict, out to be self-evident.[3]

Having stated these two principles, Mill now turns to the task of describing "What Utilitarianism Is" in Chapter Two. Like Bentham,

---

the consequences, but on something else). He says that when Kant "begins to deduce from [his Categorical Imperative] any of the actual duties of morality, he fails, almost grotesquely, to show that there would be any contradiction...in the adoption by all rational beings of the most outrageously immoral rules of conduct. All he shows is that the *consequences* of their universal adoption would be such that no one would choose to incur." (*Utilitarianism*, p. 259)

[1] *Ibid.*, p. 252.

[2] Philosophers now make a distinction between *action-based* ethicists, who see the primary task of ethics to determine how we should *act* when we find ourselves in an ethical dilemma, and *virtue-based* ethicists, who see the main task as one of determining what the person ought to *be*, what sort of *virtues* he or she should possess.

[3] *Utilitarianism*, p. 253. Ross' theory of prima facie duties, for instance, has not been widely accepted, despite the plausibility of the duties he lists, because he doesn't give a rule for deciding which duty to follow when two or more of these duties conflict.

Mill accepts Hedonism as correctly stating the proper "end" of all actions and so it forms the basis for the theory:

> [T]he theory of life on which this theory of morality is grounded ...[is] that pleasure, and freedom from pain, are the only things desirable as ends; and that all desirable things...are desirable either for the pleasure inherent in themselves, or as means to the promotion of pleasure and the prevention of pain.[1]

Mill is now able to state the "one fundamental principle" of morality which is based on the acceptance of Hedonism. The definition of Utilitarianism which he gives is no less vague than Bentham's:

> The creed which accepts as the foundation of morals, Utility, or the Greatest Happiness Principle, holds that actions are right as they tend to promote happiness, wrong as they tend to produce the reverse of happiness. By happiness is intended pleasure, and the absence of pain; by unhappiness, pain, and the privation of pleasure.[2]

Mill's principle, Utilitarianism, becomes clearer, however, as he considers seven criticisms which force him to provide more details as he responds to them.

The first criticism Mill considers finds fault with the hedonistic basis of the theory:

> To suppose that life has (as they express it) no higher end than pleasure — no better and nobler object of desire and pursuit — they designate as utterly mean and grovelling; as a doctrine worthy only of swine....[3]

Mill's response to this objection is not only a reply to these critics, but a reaction to the narrowness of Bentham's version of Hedonistic Utilitarianism as well:

---

[1] *Utilitarianism*, p. 257.

[2] *Ibid.*, p. 257.

[3] *Ibid.*, pp. 257-8.

Human beings have faculties more elevated than the animal appetites, and when once made conscious of them, do not regard anything as happiness which does not include their gratification....It is quite compatible with the principle of utility to recognize the fact, that some kinds of pleasure are more valuable than others. It would be absurd that while, in estimating all other things, quality is considered as well as quantity, the estimation of pleasures should be supposed to depend on quantity alone.[1]

Unlike Bentham, and other utilitarians, who would look for a *quantitative* basis for the presumed superiority of mental over physical pleasures — they might last longer, for instance — Mill is convinced that some pleasures are *qualitatively* superior to others. In answer to the question of what makes one pleasure qualitatively superior to others, Mill replies:

Of two pleasures, if there be one to which all or almost all who have experience of both give a decided preference...that is the more desirable pleasure. If one of the two is, by those who are competently acquainted with both, placed so far above the other that they prefer it, even though knowing it to be attended with a greater amount of discontent..., we are justified in ascribing to the preferred enjoyment a superiority in quality....[2]

It is shortly after this passage that Mill gives the famous line: "It is better to be a human being dissatisfied than a pig satisfied; better to be Socrates dissatisfied than a fool satisfied."[3]

Mill notes that many people, who were once capable of appreciating the higher pleasures, may lose that ability due to a "want of sustenance":

Capacity for the nobler feelings is in most natures a very tender plant, easily killed, not only by hostile influences, but by mere want of sustenance; and in the majority of young persons it speedily dies away if the occupations to which their

---

[1] *Utilitarianism*, pp. 258-9.

[2] *Ibid.*, p. 259.

[3] *Ibid.*, p. 260.

position in life has devoted them, and the society into which it has thrown them, are not favourable to keeping that higher capacity in exercise.[1]

These people may end up addicting themselves to physical pleasures because they are "the only ones which they are any longer capable of enjoying." Still, Mill insists that those who *are* "equally capable of appreciating and enjoying both" prefer mental pleasures to physical ones; and the "ultimate aim" of life is "an existence exempt as far as possible from pain, and as rich as possible in enjoyments, both in point of quantity and quality" for as many people as possible. Thus, society has an obligation, through education, to cultivate the "higher faculties" of human beings.

There are questions the reader is likely to have about Mill's distinction between higher and lower pleasures. Are there some pleasures (mental pleasures) which those who are capable of appreciating all types of pleasures would prefer? And, if this is the case, is it true that we cannot account for this difference in a purely quantitative manner? More importantly, has Mill abandoned Utilitarianism, as some have claimed, by introducing his qualitative distinction? I don't think so. Mill can still base the rightness and wrongness of actions entirely upon the consequences of those actions. He can look at two kinds of consequences, the amount of $pleasure_1$ (mental pleasure) and $pleasure_2$ (physical pleasure), and their opposites, which is likely to result, each unit of $pleasure_1$ being consistently weighted more than each unit of $pleasure_2$, and taking into account the intensity, duration, etc., of each, just as Bentham did. The mathematical formula for computing the right action becomes more complicated; but there can still be, in principle, a mathematical formula for doing so. Mill has not abandoned the basic idea behind Bentham's "hedonistic calculus."

Mill now turns to a second type of critic of the hedonistic aspect of Utilitarianism, one who maintains either that happiness is unattainable or that we have no right to be happy. To those who maintain that happiness is unattainable, Mill replies that even "if no happiness is to be had at all by human beings," still "something might be still said for the utilitarian theory; since utility includes not solely the pursuit of happiness, but the prevention or mitigation of unhappiness."[2] Mill

---

[1] *Utilitarianism*, p. 261.

[2] *Ibid.*, p. 263.

thinks, however, that happiness is attainable for most people. Perhaps "a continuity of highly pleasurable excitement" is impossible, because human beings seem to need both "tranquility" and "excitement"; but "a life of rapture" should not be thought of as the ideal of a happy life. Instead, he says, what is properly understood as a happy life is a life consisting of:

> moments of [rapture], in an existence made up of few and transitory pains, many and various pleasures, with a decided predominance of the active over the passive, and having as the foundation of the whole, not to expect more from life than it is capable of bestowing.[1]

The two principal obstacles for not having such an existence, according to Mill, are "want of mental cultivation" and "a sincere interest in the public good," both of which can be corrected through education.[2] Even if your own life is lacking in some respect, if you can find solace in the *general* welfare of society, perhaps even in sacrificing your own happiness for the good of all, you can feel that your life has been worthwhile:

> Though it is only in a very imperfect state of the world's arrangements that any one can best serve the happiness of others by the absolute sacrifice of his own, yet so long as the world is in that imperfect state, I fully acknowledge that the readiness to make such a sacrifice is the highest virtue which can be found in man.[3]

The answer Mill gives, then, to those who would ask "what right thou hast to be happy" is that the goal of action is not *your own* happiness, but the happiness of *all*. You should try to bring about the greatest net happiness, taking *everyone* into account. Utilitarianism is neither altruistic, nor egoistic:

---

[1] *Utilitarianism*, p. 264.

[2] Mill says: "education and opinion, which have so vast a power over human character, should so use that power as to establish in the mind of every individual an indissoluble association between his own happiness and the good of the whole...." (*Ibid.*, p. 269.)

[3] *Ibid.*, p. 267.

The utilitarian morality does recognize in human beings the power of sacrificing their own greatest good for the good of others. It only refuses to admit that the sacrifice is itself a good. A sacrifice which does not increase, or tend to increase, the sum total of happiness, it considers as wasted....[The] happiness which forms the utilitarian standard of what is right in conduct, is not the agent's own happiness, but that of all concerned. As between his own happiness and that of others, utilitarianism requires him to be as strictly impartial as a disinterested and benevolent spectator.[1]

At this point, a third objection to Utilitarianism arises. Some critics, thinking that you will on many occasions have to sacrifice your own welfare for the good of all, "find fault with its standard as being too high for humanity." But Mill correctly points out that a good ethical theory is supposed to give us an ideal towards which to aspire. He also notes that the utilitarian theory does not require you to have a benevolent motive for your action: "the motive has nothing to do with the morality of the action."[2] You might have a self-interested motive, but as long as you do the action which is likely to result in the best consequences for all, you are acting correctly: "The great majority of good actions are intended not for the benefit of the world, but for that of individuals...."[3] Finally, Mill points out that few of us are put in the situation where our actions will affect a large number of other people, so it is unlikely that you will often have to sacrifice your own happiness for the general good.

Fourth, Mill considers the objection that "utilitarianism renders men cold and unsympathising." Mill's answer is that it is true of any (action-based) ethical theory that your action will be evaluated according to whether you followed the correct principle or not, not whether you are likable. But he points out, just as he wanted to say to Bentham, that "there are other things which interest us in persons besides the rightness and wrongness of their actions."[4] I would add that a theory which takes into account the happiness and unhappiness of others, in deciding how one should act, is hardly "cold and unsympathizing." It is true, however, that you should not "play

---

[1] *Utilitarianism*, p. 268.

[2] *Ibid.*, p. 270.

[3] *Ibid.*

[4] *Ibid.*, p. 271.

favorites," by attaching more weight to the happiness of some than to others. There is an objectivity to the utilitarian ideal which most would consider admirable.

The fifth criticism of Utilitarianism which Mill considers is that it is said to be "a *godless* doctrine." Here Mill correctly states that it is possible to believe in God and attempt to give an ethical principle which we all should follow. This amounts to "interpret[ing] to us the will of God." As he says later in the book, the utilitarian principle can easily be viewed as the principle which God would like us to follow:

> [I]f men believe, as most profess to do, in the goodness of God, those who think that conduciveness to the general happiness is the essence, or even only the criterion of good, must necessarily believe that it is also that which God approves.[1]

The sixth criticism raises a practical problem with Utilitarianism: "there is not time, previous to action, for calculating and weighing the effects of any line of conduct on the general happiness." Mill, ever the champion of inductive reasoning, points out that we can make educated predictions as to the likely consequences of our actions since:

> During [the whole past duration of the human species], mankind have been learning by experience the tendencies of actions; on which experience all the prudence, as well as all the morality of life, are dependent.[2]

Our past experience has led us to form general rules of thumb, for instance that lying and stealing are wrong. We have learned from experience that, in general, these actions do not lead to the best consequences; so, when pressed for time, we can rely on these rules of thumb to make quick decisions about how we should act. This does not mean that following these rules of thumb is *always* likely to lead to the best consequences. There can be exceptions. If we find ourselves in a situation which we think might be such an exception, and we have the time, we should certainly try to calculate the likely effects of the *particular* action instead of relying on the rules of thumb.[3]

---

[1] *Utilitarianism*, p. 280.

[2] *Ibid.*, p. 275.

[3] It is because Mill allows us to break these rules of thumb, when it is

The seventh, and last, objection Mill considers in Chapter Two against Utilitarianism is that:

> [A] utilitarian will be apt to make his own particular case an exception...and, when under temptation, will see a utility in the breach of a rule, greater than he will see in its observance.[1]

But Mill points out that Utilitarianism is not "the only creed which is able to furnish us with excuses for evil doing." Any ethical theory can be abused, but it is hardly a criticism of the theory that someone might not follow it.

In Chapter Three, Mill, like Bentham had before him, considers the sanctions — that is, the pressures that can be put upon individuals or that exist naturally — to influence them to follow the principle of utility. He begins the discussion by asking:

> [W]hy am I bound to promote the general happiness? If my own happiness lies in something else, why may I not give that the preference?[2]

There are the usual sanctions which can be appealed to, like "the hope of favour and the fear of displeasure, from our fellow creatures or from the Ruler of the Universe," to motivate people to do the right thing when it conflicts with self-interest. Mill maintains that there is "no reason why these motives for observance should not attach themselves to the utilitarian morality, as completely and powerfully as to any other."[3] He points out, though, that these are *external* sanctions. More effective would be an *internal* sanction, something lying within individuals themselves, which would cause them to do the right action. Conscience, or a "feeling of duty," should play this role. Mill believes that "the moral feelings are not innate, but acquired." Education is the key to making sure that we have the right feelings:

---

likely to lead to better consequences to do so, that he should be considered to be an *act*, rather than *rule*, utilitarian. (See Mark Strasser, *The Moral Philosophy of John Stuart Mill, Towards Modifications of Contemporary Utilitarianism*, Longwood Academic Press, Wakefield, New Hampshire, 1991, pp. 25-7.

[1] *Utilitarianism*, p. 277.

[2] *Ibid.*, p. 279.

[3] *Ibid.*, p. 280.

[B]y the improvement of education, the feeling of unity with our fellow-creatures shall be...as deeply rooted in our character, and to our own consciousness as completely a part of our nature, as the horror of crime is in an ordinary well brought up young person.[1]

But even without a proper education, Mill argues that there is a strong *natural* basis for accepting the utilitarian morality. It is this which provides the "ultimate sanction" for Utilitarianism:

But there is this basis of powerful natural sentiment; and this it is which...will constitute the strength of the utilitarian morality. This firm foundation is that of the social feelings of mankind; the desire to be in unity with our fellow-creatures.... The social state is at once so natural, so necessary, and so habitual to man, that, except in some unusual circumstances or by an effort of voluntary abstraction, he never conceives himself otherwise than as a member of a body....[2]

We need other people, our lives are inextricably bound up with theirs, and "this association is riveted more and more, as mankind are further removed from the state of savage independence." Mill argues that the only possible way to live in harmony with our fellow human beings is for us to take everyone's interests equally into account: "Society between equals can only exist on the understanding that the interests of all are to be regarded equally."[3]

Since there is a natural sentiment which inclines us towards accepting Utilitarianism, and since the principle can be reinforced though education as well as public opinion, what Mill would like to see is:

this feeling of unity to be taught as a religion, and the whole force of education, of institutions, and of opinion, directed, as it once was in the case of religion, to make every person grow up from infancy surrounded on all sides both by the profession and practice of [Utilitarianism]....[4]

---

[1] *Utilitarianism*, pp. 288-9.

[2] *Ibid.*, p 284.

[3] *Ibid.*, p. 285.

[4] *Ibid.*, p. 286.

Chapter Four of *Utilitarianism* is titled "Of What Sort of Proof the Principle of Utility is Susceptible." It actually contains a defense of only the *hedonistic* part of his theory of Utilitarianism.[1] In this chapter Mill doesn't adhere to his, and Bentham's, official position that "questions of ultimate ends do not admit of proof."[2] Mill clearly gives an argument for the first part of the hedonistic view, that "all pleasure (or happiness) is intrinsically good," and, unfortunately, it is extremely weak. Here is the argument he gives:

> [T]he sole evidence it is possible to produce that anything is desirable, is that people do actually desire it....each person, so far as he believes it to be attainable, desires his own happiness. This, however, being a fact, we have not only all the proof which the case admits of, but all which it is possible to require, that happiness is a good....[3]

It is generally acknowledged that this argument commits the *naturalistic fallacy*, that is, it attempts to derive an "ought" statement from an "is" statement. He is saying that because people *do* desire happiness, they *ought* to (it is desirable).

Mill's initial attempt to convince us of the second claim that the hedonist makes, that *"only* pleasure (or happiness) is intrinsically good," is more plausible. It is not actually an argument, but an explanation of how it could be true that, while we value other things, their value lies in their relationship to pleasure (or happiness). He says that other things which we value, like health or money, are initially thought of as valuable because they lead to pleasure (or happiness). After a while, we may think of them as desirable in and of themselves, but their real value still lies in their connection with pleasure (or happiness). We may say of each of these *instrumental* goods:

---

[1] We can think of Chapters Three and Four together as providing a defense of the *full* theory of Hedonistic Utilitarianism, Chapter Three defending the general position that we should calculate what is likely to lead to the best consequences for *everyone* and Chapter Four defending the view that the only consequences we should consider are the units of *pleasure*, and its opposite, which are likely to result.

[2] *Utilitarianism*, p. 288.

[3] *Ibid.*, p. 288.

From being a means to happiness, it has come to be itself a principal ingredient of the individual's conception of happiness....What was once desired as an instrument for the attainment of happiness, has come to be desired for its own sake. In being desired for its own sake it is, however, desired as *part* of happiness. The person is made, or thinks he would be made, happy by its mere possession; and made unhappy by failure to obtain it. The desire of it is not a different thing from the desire of happiness....[1]

Mill is apparently not content, however, with this explanation as a defense of the hedonist's second claim, that pleasure is the only thing which is intrinsically good. Once again he tries to *prove* the claim. Mill attempts to equate "desiring a thing" with "finding it pleasant":

I believe that...desiring a thing and finding it pleasant, aversion to it and thinking of it as painful, are phenomena entirely inseparable, or rather two parts of the same phenomenon; in strictness of language, two different modes of naming the same psychological fact: that to think of an object as desirable...and to think of it as pleasant, are one and the same thing; and that to desire anything, except in proportion as the idea of it is pleasant, is a physical and metaphysical impossibility.[2]

Is it necessarily true that a person who desires something finds it pleasant? I might desire to have a frank discussion with a colleague with whom I am at odds, just to clear the air, but that doesn't mean that the prospect is pleasant to me. Similarly, I might desire that my son return an item he has stolen to the owner of the store from which he has taken it, but that doesn't mean that I find the idea of my son begging for mercy and resenting me for making him do the right thing to be pleasant.

Chapter Four of *Utilitarianism* may be weak, but little damage is done to Mill's overall philosophy. He should not have attempted to prove Hedonism; and even if Hedonism is incorrect, the general view of Utilitarianism can still be accepted, since one need not be a hedonist

---

[1] *Utilitarianism*, p. 291.

[2] *Ibid.*, pp. 292-3.

to be a utilitarian[1]. In any case, the concluding chapter of *Utilitarianism*, "On the Connection Between Justice and Utility," more than makes up for any deficiencies in the chapter before. It is a *tour de force*.

The main criticism people have of Utilitarianism, which Mill saves for the last chapter, is that it cannot adequately account for important considerations of justice. Indeed, they fear that following the theory could lead to acts of injustice, in particular the violation of people's rights. Most philosophers accept the following picture of the relationship between the right action, what serves utility, what is just, what shows proper respect for people's rights and what people deserve[2]:

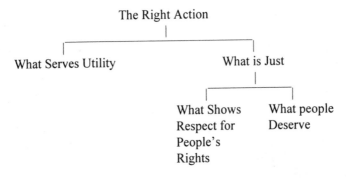

The Right Action

What Serves Utility   What is Just

What Shows Respect for People's Rights   What people Deserve

Doing the right action involves taking into account both what serves utility and what is just, where the justice component also involves two distinct considerations. What shows respect for people's rights is different from what people deserve because one has rights, and here we are talking about *moral* rights, just in virtue of the fact that one is a certain type of being, whereas what one deserves depends upon one's past behavior.

Consider the following example: You run an exclusive clinic in a remote area, servicing important people who need health care and

---

[1] One could, for instance, be a *pluralistic* utilitarian and take into account other consequences, in addition to the pleasure which is likely to result, in trying to determine which action is likely to result in the greatest net good consequences, considering all those affected.

[2] See, for instance, James Rachels, "What People Deserve," in John Arthur and William Shaw, editors, *Justice and Economic Distribution*, Prentice Hall, Englewood Cliffs, N. J., 1978.

desire privacy. You are able to offer your clients the best care that money can buy. It so happens that you have three important people (perhaps the world's most renowned violinist, a Pulitzer prize winning author, and a greatly admired political leader) in your clinic at the moment who require organ transplants (different organs are involved) or they will die shortly. You have canvassed the world over and cannot find suitable organs. The problem is that they all, coincidentally, have the same extremely rare tissue type, a match is needed for a successful transplant, and no one has died recently with that tissue type. But you happen to have a lowly janitor working for you who has that rare tissue type (you keep detailed information on all your employees). You could arrange an "accident" for the janitor and then his body could be used to save all three of the "important" people. (The janitor has no family who will inquire about his death and you routinely sign death certificates.) It would seem that what serves *utility* is to kill the janitor to save the three other people whose lives positively affect so many others; but it also seems clear that this is not *just*. Surely the janitor has a *right* to life. (To see that the other consideration of justice, *desert*, might conflict with the *rights* consideration, imagine that the janitor is a murderer who happened to go free on a technicality.)

In Chapter Five of *Utilitarianism* Mill gives a powerful argument, to counter his critics, that the following picture is the correct view of the relationship between the right action, what serves utility and what is just:

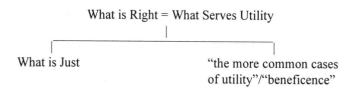

Mill argues that justice, "which is grounded on utility," is "the chief part, and incomparably the most sacred and binding part, of all morality."[1] It is a branch of "social utility" which is "vastly more important, and therefore more absolute and imperative" — and, as a result, thought of "not only as different in degree, but also in kind"[2] — than "the more common cases of utility" or acts of "beneficence."

---

[1] *Utilitarianism*, p. 315.

[2] *Ibid.*, p. 321.

How does Mill argue that justice is a branch of what serves utility? He first attempts "to ascertain what is the distinguishing character of justice." In particular, he tries to determine whether there is a common quality to all the actions which are "designated as unjust (for justice, like many other moral attributes, is best defined by its opposite)."[1] Which actions are considered to be unjust? It is unjust, he says, to violate the *legal* and *moral* rights of anyone. The two are distinct because it is possible to have an unjust law, and when that happens it is because the law infringes upon a moral right of someone. It is also unjust to not give people what they *deserve*, where "a person is understood to deserve good if he does right, evil if he does wrong." It is unjust to "*break faith* with any one" and, finally, it is unjust to "be *partial*: to show favour or preference to one person over another, in matters to which favour and preference do not properly apply."[2] Mill points out that it is not always wrong to do these things, since each one might, on occasion, be "overruled by a stronger obligation of justice."

Mill now asks, what is common to all these cases of injustice? His answer is that a *right* has been violated. This is what makes justice considerations different from other moral obligations:

> It seems to me that this feature in the case — a right in some person, correlative to the moral obligation — constitutes the specific difference between justice, and generosity or beneficence. Justice implies something which is not only right to do, and wrong not to do, but which some individual person can claim from us as his moral right. No one has a moral right to our generosity or beneficence, because we are not morally bound to practise those virtues towards any given individual.[3]

There is a further element of injustice, Mill points out; but it is not unique to injustice, but rather is true of any violation of morality: "the desire to punish a person who has done harm."

> For the truth is, that the idea of penal sanction, which is the essence of law, enters not only into the conception of injustice, but into that of any kind of wrong. We do not call

---

[1] *Utilitarianism*, p. 297.
[2] *Ibid.*, pp. 298-300.
[3] *Ibid.*, p. 305.

anything wrong, unless we mean to imply that a person ought to be punished in some way or other for doing it....[1]

If it is the violation of a *right* which is the particular feature that makes an act unjust, what exactly is a "right"? Mill's answer is that:

> When we call anything a person's right, we mean that he has a valid claim on society to protect him in the possession of it, either by the force of law, or by that of education and opinion.[2]

Someone is bound to ask: But *why* should society defend people's rights; what is the basis for them? "I can give him no other reason than general utility," says Mill. Anticipating a dissatisfaction with this answer, that it doesn't account for "the strength of the obligation" when we talk about justice, Mill gets to the heart of the matter:

> If that expression ["general utility"] does not seem to convey a sufficient feeling of the strength of the obligation, nor account for the peculiar energy of the feeling, it is because there goes to the composition of the sentiment, not a rational only, but also an animal element, the thirst for retaliation; and this thirst derives its intensity, as well as its moral justification, from the extraordinarily important and impressive kind of utility which is concerned. The interest involved is that of security, to every one's feelings the most vital of all interests.[3]

So rights, and therefore justice, considerations involve our *security* which, "after physical nutriment," is the most vital need we have: "security no human being can possibly do without ."[4] Mill does seem to have found a powerful utilitarian basis for the concept of rights, and, as a result, justice. And because there is such a strong need for security in human beings, rights are not easily overridden. It would take the violation of others' rights, or the honoring of the right leading to a

---

[1] *Utilitarianism*, pp. 303-4.

[2] *Ibid.*, p. 309.

[3] *Ibid.*, pp. 309-10.

[4] *Ibid.*, p. 310.

catastrophe, to justify the violation of a right. This accords with our intuitions about rights.[1]

Mill also mentions an important advantage which his account of justice (rights) has which its rival — that justice is conceptually basic, resting on its own intuitions — lacks. People have very different intuitions about what is just:

> Some Communists consider it unjust that the produce of the labour of the community should be shared on any other principle than that of exact equality; others think it just that those should receive most whose wants are greatest; while others hold that those who work harder, or who produce more, or whose services are more valuable to the community, may justly claim a larger quota in the division of the produce.[2]

It would seem that, according to the view that intuitions about justice are fundamental, the "choice between them must be arbitrary." Mill's view, on the other hand, can, in principle, settle the matter: "Social utility alone can decide the preference."[3]

Mill appears to have found a way to respond to the central criticism of Utilitarianism — that the theory has no place for the concept of justice and can even support acts of injustice — and, in doing so, he has given us a plausible foundation for the concept of justice, as well as giving us a way to settle disputes about what is just. Chapter Five of Mill's *Utilitarianism*, it seems to me, is one of the most ambitious and important chapters in a work of philosophy ever written.

There is, however, one small problem with Mill's conceptual analysis. Although he discusses both rights and desert in connection with justice, it is unclear whether he sees them as distinct components of justice or whether he believes that to be treated as we deserve to be treated is one of our rights. On the one hand, when he itemizes types of injustices, he distinguishes between violating people's moral rights and not treating people as they deserve to be treated. Yet Mill also says that all acts of injustice involve violations of people's moral rights, which would lead us to think that he sees not treating people as they deserve

---

[1] See, for instance, Ronald Dworkin, *Taking Rights Seriously*, Harvard University Press, Cambridge, Mass., 1977, pp. 184-205.

[2] *Utilitarianism*, p. 301.

[3] *Ibid.*, p. 314.

to be treated as a violation of a moral right. The inconsistency is somewhat troubling, but either view is plausible.

Study Questions

1. Do you agree with Mill that some pleasures are *qualitatively* superior to others? What is his basis for determining which ones are qualitatively superior?

2. How can it be said that Utilitarianism is neither egoistic nor altruistic?

3. What are the criticisms of Utilitarianism which Mill considers in Chapter Two of *Utilitarianism*? Are you satisfied with his responses?

4. What is the "powerful natural sentiment" which, according to Mill, provides the "ultimate sanction" for Utilitarianism?

5. How does Mill defend the hedonistic aspect of his theory? Why have some found this to be the weakest part of *Utilitarianism*?

6. What does Mill attempt to prove in the last chapter of *Utilitarianism*?

7. How does Mill connect rights/justice with utility?

4

On Liberty

In *Utilitarianism*, Mill argued that the principle of utility is the ultimate principle of morality, that those actions are right which are likely to result in the greatest net pleasure (or happiness), considering both the quantity and quality of the pleasures, or the least displeasure, taking everyone affected into account. In *On Liberty*, as we shall see, Mill is worried about the "tyranny of the majority." He is anxious to enlarge the sphere of individual liberty, seeming to allow individuals the right to act in ways which are not likely to result in the greatest net pleasure for all. It has appeared to many as if two different authors had written *Utilitarianism* and *On Liberty*, that Mill is contradicting himself in his two most famous works. Let us see exactly what he says in *On Liberty* and whether it is consistent with what he has said in *Utilitarianism*.

Mill asserts in the introduction to *On Liberty*, first, that: "The subject of this Essay is...Civil, or Social Liberty: the nature and limits of the power which can be legitimately exercised by society over the individual."[1] This work, then, is concerned with what we would call Social or Political Philosophy. It deals with the relationship between the government, those in power, and citizens. This is important to note because Mill is not attempting in this work, as he attempted in

---

[1] *On Liberty*, in Warnock, New American Library, New York, 1974, p. 126.

Utilitarianism, to give a complete account of morality, but, rather, restrict his discussion to the proper relationship between the state, as the representative of society as a whole, and individual citizens.

Mill begins his discussion of Social/Political Philosophy by noting that once those who fought for liberty were concerned about the rulers having too much power over citizens, and so their aim was "to set limits to the power which the ruler should be suffered to exercise over the community." Over the years, the defenders of liberty managed to establish that citizens have *rights* and, later, instituted "constitutional checks, by which the consent of the community, or of a body of some sort, supposed to represent its interests, was made a necessary condition to some of the more important acts of the governing power."[1] This eventually led to establishing democracies: "It appeared to them much better that the various magistrates of the State should be [the people's] tenants or delegates, revocable at their pleasure."[2] It was thought, when this was achieved, that since the rulers were now under the control of the people, that abuse of power problems had been solved: "The nation did not need to be protected against itself."

Mill points out, however, that:

> The will of the people...practically means the will of the most numerous, or the most active *part* of the people; the majority, or those who succeed in making themselves accepted as the majority; the people, consequently *may* desire to oppress a part of their number; and precautions are as much needed against this as against any other abuse of power...."[T]he tyranny of the majority" is now generally included among the evils against which society requires to be on its guard....[The majority] practices a social tyranny more formidable than many kinds of political oppression, since, though not usually upheld by such extreme penalties, it leaves fewer means of escape, penetrating much more deeply into the details of life, and enslaving the soul itself.[3]

Mill wants, in *On Liberty*, to establish that "there is a limit to the legitimate interference of collective opinion with individual

---

[1] *On Liberty*, p. 127.

[2] *Ibid.*

[3] *Ibid.*, pp. 129-30.

independence."[1] The "practical question," he says, is "where to place the limit."

Concerning the question of how extensively the government, which represents collective opinion, should be involved in citizens' lives, Mill acknowledges that there are two popular extreme positions:

> Some, whenever they see any good to be done, or evil to be remedied, would willingly instigate the government to undertake the business; while others prefer to bear almost any amount of social evil, rather than add one to the departments of human interests amenable to governmental control.[2]

The first position is associated with the philosophy of Collectivism and the second with Individualism[3].

It would appear that Mill is siding with the latter group, and in agreement with Individualism, since the principle he wishes to defend in *On Liberty*, the "object of this Essay," is the following:

> That principle is, that the sole end for which mankind are warranted, individually or collectively, in interfering with the liberty of action of any of their number, is self-protection. That the only purpose for which power can be rightfully exercised over any member of a civilised community, against his will, is to prevent harm to others. His own good, either physical or moral, is not a sufficient warrant....The only part of the conduct of any one, for which he is amenable to society, is that which concerns others. In the part which merely concerns himself, his independence is, of right, absolute. Over himself, over his own body and mind, the individual is sovereign.[4]

---

[1] *On Liberty*, p. 130.

[2] *Ibid.*, p. 134.

[3] Or Libertarianism, which is the political version of the more general philosophy of Individualism. Libertarians see government interference in our lives as the source of most of our ills and, therefore, advocate a minimal government only to protect individual rights instead of providing positive goods for society.

[4] *On Liberty*, p. 135.

Mill adds just two qualifications, that "we are not speaking of children," who need to be taken care of by others, and:

> For the same reason, we may leave out of consideration those backwards states of society in which the race itself may be considered as in its nonage....Despotism is a legitimate mode of government in dealing with barbarians, provided the end be their improvement, and the means justified by actually effecting that end.[1]

The last qualification should make us suspicious of whether Mill is, indeed, giving a defense of the classic individualist, or libertarian, position. The next thing he says is proof that he is not:

> It is proper to state that I forego any advantage which could be derived to my argument from the idea of abstract right, as a thing independent of utility. I regard utility as the ultimate appeal on all ethical questions....[2]

Typically, an individualist will argue that individuals have a *right* to live their lives as they choose, as long as they allow others to do the same (i.e., they don't harm others in the process). It may appear that Mill is saying that we do *not* have a *right* to live our lives as we please as long as we do not harm others. But this is not true. He has argued, in Chapter Five of *Utilitarianism*, that we do have rights; but they are not logically primitive. They are grounded in utility. Mill only rejects the idea of "*abstract* right."[3] The first sentence is not necessarily, then, a problem for the individualist. The real problem with this passage, for the individualist, lies in the last sentence.

In saying that "utility [is] the ultimate appeal on all ethical questions," Mill is maintaining that the goal of social and political policies is the welfare of *all* (i.e., the greatest number), not the individual. If it turns out that it is not likely to be in the interest of all to allow people to live their lives as they choose, as long as they don't harm others, then this policy should *not* be advocated. Mill's view is, therefore, not consistent with true Individualism which aims for the good of the *individual*, rather than society.

---

[1] *On Liberty*, pp. 135-6.

[2] *Ibid.*, p. 136.

[3] My italics.

How can Mill be saying the sorts of things which an individualist would say, and a collectivist would not — that he is concerned about "the tyranny of the majority" and that individuals should be allowed to do anything they want as long as they don't harm others — yet also be saying that "the ultimate appeal on all ethical questions" is a collectivist principle? Immediately after stating that he "regard[s] utility as the ultimate appeal on all ethical questions," Mill adds something which explains how he thinks he can defend individualistic policies by appealing to social utility:

> it must be utility in the largest sense, grounded on the permanent interests of man as a progressive being. Those interests, I contend, authorise the subjection of individual spontaneity to external control, only in respect to those actions of each, which concern the interests of other people.[1]

Mill is maintaining here that we must not only consider the consequences of our policies for all *existing* human beings, but look to the *future* as well. We must consider that human beings are capable of, and ought to, evolve into *better* human beings; we should try to bring this about. We cannot just consider what the majority of the people who currently exist would want, but rather what is likely to lead to more people enjoying qualitatively and quantitatively superior pleasures in the future. The desires of people who currently exist may be very narrowly self-interested, because we as a society have failed to educate them to appreciate the higher pleasures in life and to identify their own interests with the public good, so we have to look to the future in deciding what would be best for humanity in the long run.

Mill's position seems to be that individualist policies are likely to lead to a better society in the long run. The *goal* is what is best for *humanity*, not what's best for the individual; but individualist policies are the best *means* to achieve this goal. If this interpretation is correct, then Mill is consistently a collectivist; but he advocates individualist policies to achieve his collectivist aim. In this way Mill escapes the contradiction which he is accused of; and he may also have found a way to reconcile Individualism and Collectivism, to cut through the debate between them. Let us see if this reading of Mill is consistent with the rest of what he says in *On Liberty*.

---

[1] *On Liberty*, p. 136.

There are three particular areas in which Mill thinks citizens should have liberty: (1) "the inward domain of consciousness" and "the liberty of expressing and publishing opinions," (2) "liberty of tastes and pursuits; of framing the plan of [their lives] to suit [their] own character," and (3) the "freedom to unite, for any purpose not involving harm to others: the persons combining being supposed to be of full age, and not forced or deceived." Mill will go on to argue at length, in the rest of the book, why citizens should have these freedoms. He does make it clear, though, even in this introduction, that he will be giving a utilitarian defense: "Mankind are greater gainers by suffering each other to live as seems good to themselves, than by compelling each to live as seems good to the rest."[1]

Chapter Two, "Of the Liberty of Thought and Discussion," contains an extended utilitarian argument in favor of citizens being permitted to express any opinions[2] they wish. Essentially it is a separation of cases argument. Mill argues that in each possible case where someone might wish to express a view, while society would like to prevent the view from being heard, it is to society's benefit to let the person speak. Mill considers three possible cases: When the speaker is right and society is wrong in its view, when the speaker is wrong and society is correct; and, finally, when both the speaker and society are partially correct in their views, when they "share the truth between them."

Before discussing the three cases, Mill makes two preliminary comments. One shows how strongly he feels about individuals having the right to express their views:

> If all mankind minus one were of one opinion, and only one person were of the contrary opinion, mankind would be no more justified in silencing that one person, than he, if he had the power, would be justified in silencing mankind.[3]

---

[1] *On Liberty*, p. 138.

[2] It is significant to note that Mill is talking about expressing opinions and not free speech in general. It may be desirable that there be restrictions on *other* types of speech — such as yelling "Fire!" in a crowded theater when there is none — which would not be classified as expressions of opinion.

[3] *On Liberty*, p. 142.

The other shows that Mill will be giving a utilitarian defense of the right to express opinions, and it also gives us a good idea of what his argument will be for the first two cases:

> [T]he peculiar evil of silencing the expression of an opinion is, that it is robbing the human race; posterity as well as the existing generation; those who dissent from the opinion, still more than those who hold it. If the opinion is right, they are deprived of the opportunity of exchanging error for truth; if wrong, they lose, what is almost as great a benefit, the clear perception and livelier impression of truth, produced by its collision with error.[1]

The first case Mill considers is that "the opinion which it is attempted to suppress by authority may possibly be true." Mill hastens to add that "those who desire to suppress it, of course deny its truth; but they are not infallible." The last part is important. As Mill says: "All silencing of discussion is an assumption of infallibility."[2] But history shows that we are not infallible: "History teems with instances of truth being put down by persecution." Mill reminds us that Socrates and Jesus, two of the wisest and best individuals who ever lived, were put to death for their beliefs.

Mill says that it is fine to hold a view which has not yet been refuted to be true, but:

> There is the greatest difference between presuming an opinion to be true, because, with every opportunity for contesting it, it has not been refuted, and assuming its truth for the purpose of not permitting its refutation.[3]

Unless we permit, and seriously consider, challenges to the views which we think are correct, we cannot be sure whether our views are really true or whether we are just asserting them dogmatically.

Obviously if a view which someone wishes to express is true, even if the rest of us don't want to hear it, it is to our benefit to let it be expressed. Mill, also, points out that we lose a great deal if the climate

---

[1] *On Liberty*, pp. 142-3.

[2] *Ibid.*, p. 143.

[3] *Ibid.*, p. 145.

is such that individuals are afraid to express views which the public considers unacceptable:

> Who can compute what the world loses in the multitude of promising intellects combined with timid characters, who dare not follow out any bold, vigorous, independent train of thought, lest it should land them in something which would admit of being considered irreligious or immoral?...where the discussion of the greatest questions which can occupy humanity is considered to be closed, we cannot hope to find that generally high scale of mental activity which has made some periods of history so remarkable.[1]

Mill now turns to the hardest case, when the opinion to be expressed is false and the rest of us have the correct view. How is it to our benefit to let a false view be expressed? Mill's answer is that however true our view may be, "if it is not fully, frequently, and fearlessly discussed, it will be held as a dead dogma, not a living truth."[2] Individuals who have opposing views challenge us to think about *why* our views are correct. Unless we can argue for our beliefs, which includes being able to defend them against objections, "truth ...is but one superstition the more." As Mill says, "he who knows only his side of the case, knows little of that."[3]

Some will say that it is sufficient that we learn from teachers what the opposing views are and how to refute them, but Mill replies that it is necessary "to hear [opposing views] from persons who actually believe them; who defend them in earnest, and do their very utmost for them."[4] Mill is, further, convinced that unless we understand the perspectives of our opponents, we don't really know what our own views *mean*:

> [N]ot only the grounds of the opinion are forgotten in the absence of discussion, but too often the meaning of the opinion itself....Instead of a vivid conception and a living belief, there remain only a few phrases retained by rote....[5]

---

[1] *On Liberty*, pp. 160-1.

[2] *Ibid.*, p. 161.

[3] *Ibid.*, p. 163.

[4] *Ibid.*

[5] *Ibid.*, p. 166.

As an example, Mill points out that contemporary Christians only pay lip-service to the things they claim to believe, "that the blessed are the poor and humble," "that they should judge not, lest they be judged," "that they should love their neighbour as themselves," etcetera. Growing up in a land where these views are not criticized, Christians no longer understand their meaning; they have ceased to be "living beliefs which regulate conduct." "Both teachers and learners go to sleep at their post, as soon as there is no enemy in the field."[1]

The last case, which Mill says is more common than either of the first two cases, is:

> when the conflicting doctrines, instead of one being true and the other false, share the truth between them; and the nonconforming opinion is needed to supply the remainder of the truth, of which the received doctrine embodies only a part. ...Popular opinions...are often true, but seldom, or never the whole truth.[2]

Once again, it is beneficial that the "nonconforming" opinion be expressed, because it contains a part of the truth which we need to hear. The truth very often, according to Mill, is arrived at as a result of "the reconciling and combining of opposites." For a time, one extreme view may be dominant, then the opposite extreme view becomes popular, but the truth lies somewhere in the middle.

Mill, once again, uses Christianity as his example. He argues that Christian morality is an extreme view, containing something of the truth, which could use some correcting from an opposing viewpoint:

> Christian morality (so called) has all the characters of a reaction; it is, in great part, a protest against Paganism. Its ideal is negative rather than positive; passive rather than active;...in its precepts (as has been well said) "thou shalt not" predominates unduly over "thou shalt." In its horror of sensuality, it has made an idol of asceticism....It is essentially a doctrine of passive obedience.... [W]hatever exists of magnanimity, highmindedness, personal dignity, even the sense of honour, is derived from the purely human, not the religious part of our education, and could never have grown

[1] *On Liberty*, p. 170.
[2] *Ibid.*, p. 173.

out of a standard of ethics in which the only worth, professedly recognized, is that of obedience....[A] large portion of the noblest and most valuable moral teaching has been the work, not only of men who did not know, but of men who knew and rejected, the Christian faith.[1]

Some critics have objected to Mill's argument — which permits the expression of any opinion, no matter how objectionable it may seem to society — on the grounds that "Mill treats human beings as disinterested reasoning machines, with no vital emotional interests at stake in the subject under dispute."[2] Mill would respond that it is better for humanity, in the long run, that conditions be such that the truth is likely to emerge, rather than encouraging people to retain their prejudices. But Mill certainly does not discount the emotions and their effects on others. He hasn't said that people who find certain views to be offensive must be forced to listen to them. He is merely arguing that if we have to choose between a policy of permitting the free expression of opinions or not, that the first is more likely to serve "the permanent interests of man as a progressive being" than the latter.

Chapter Three of *On Liberty*, titled "Of Individuality, as One of the Elements of Well-Being," is a utilitarian argument in favor of citizens being permitted to *act* as they please — which includes being able to live their lives as they choose and unite with whomever they wish — as long as they don't harm others. Mill begins by clearly stating that "no one pretends that actions should be as free as opinions." Nevertheless, he will argue that it is beneficial, "in things which do not primarily concern others, [that] individuality should assert itself." Mill sees being able to live our lives as we please as "one of the principle ingredients of human happiness, and quite the chief ingredient of individual and social progress."[3]

Mill recognizes that the majority of currently existing human beings may not appreciate individuality; they may even find it threatening:

> The majority, being satisfied with the ways of mankind as they now are (for it is they who make them what they are),

---

[1] *On Liberty*, pp. 177-9.

[2] Andrew Pyle, *Liberty, Contemporary Responses to John Stuart Mill*, Thoemmes Press, Bristol, England, 1994, p. xix.

[3] *On Liberty*, p. 185.

cannot comprehend why those ways should not be good enough for everybody; and what is more, spontaneity forms no part of the ideal of the majority of moral and social reformers, but is rather looked on with jealousy, as a troublesome and perhaps rebellious obstruction to the general acceptance of what these reformers, in their own judgment, think would be best for mankind.[1]

Nevertheless, Mill thinks that it is in the long-term interest of mankind to allow individuality to flourish, since it is the source of originality from which we all derive benefits and it allows us to develop more fully as human beings.

In this chapter, Mill contrasts the typical member of "the majority" of his day unfavorably with a person who expresses his individuality:

> He who lets the world, or his own portion of it, choose his plan of life for him [as the majority do], has no need of any other faculty than the ape-like one of imitation. He who chooses his plan for himself, employs all his faculties.[2]

> [For the majority,] the mind itself is bowed to the yoke; even in what people do for pleasure, conformity is the first thing thought of; they like in crowds; they exercise choice only among things commonly done; peculiarity of taste, eccentricity of conduct, are shunned equally with crimes, until by dint of not following their own nature they have no nature to follow; their human capacities are withered and starved....[3]

Mill asks, shortly after this last passage: "Now is this, or is it not, the desirable condition of human nature?" Mill is consistently interested in what furthers the growth of human beings; and it seems to him that it is individuality, not conformity, which does so:

> It is not by watering down into uniformity all that is individual in themselves, but by cultivating it, and calling it forth, within the limits imposed by the rights and interests of

---

[1] *On Liberty*, pp. 185-6.

[2] *Ibid.*, p. 187.

[3] *Ibid.*, p. 190.

72

others, that human beings become a noble and beautiful object of contemplation....[1]

Against those who would appeal to religion to support conformity, Mill remarks:

> [I]f it be any part of religion to believe that man was made by a good Being, it is more consistent with that faith to believe that this Being gave all human faculties that they might be cultivated and unfolded, not rooted out and consumed....[2]

What we should strive for is not superior individual human beings *for their own sake*,[3] but, rather, a *better society*. This can be achieved, according to Mill, only if the individuals of which society is composed make the most of their own unique abilities:

> In proportion to the development of his individuality, each person becomes more valuable to himself, and is *therefore capable of being more valuable to others*. There is a greater fullness of life about his own existence, and when there is more life in the units *there is more in the mass* which is composed of them.[4]

Mill anticipates that there will be those who are not capable of looking to the future, not able to appreciate the long-term good consequences of encouraging individuality. They want to know how Mill's more "developed human beings are of some use to the undeveloped," i.e. themselves, who exist *now*. Mill claims that, almost by definition, they can't see the need of originality:

> Originality is the one thing which unoriginal minds cannot feel the use of. They cannot see what it is to do for them; how

---

[1] *On Liberty*, p. 102.

[2] *Ibid.*, p. 191.

[3] Note the contrast between Mill, the collectivist, and Nietzsche, the individualist, on this point. For Nietzsche, the goal of life should be to produce superior *individuals*.

[4] *Ibid.*, p. 192. Italics are mine.

should they? If they could see what it would do for them, it would not be originality.[1]

Still, Mill points out that "they might possibly learn something from" those who are original. Even if few "original" human beings make great contributions to society, because "persons of genius...are always likely to be a small minority," Mill maintains that "in order to have them, it is necessary to preserve the soil in which they grow."[2]

Chapter Four, "Of the Limits to the Authority of Society Over the Individual," is the crucial chapter of *On Liberty*. It is in this chapter that Mill tackles the central question of when we can be said to be harming others. This question must be answered in order to determine how much liberty we ought to have, since Mill maintains that we should be able to do what we want *as long as we don't harm others*.

Some will insist that the distinction Mill wishes to draw between "the part of a person's life which concerns only himself, and that which concerns others" doesn't exist:

> How (it may be asked) can any part of the conduct of a member of society be a matter of indifference to the other members? No person is an entirely isolated being; it is impossible for a person to do anything seriously or permanently hurtful to himself, without mischief reaching at least to his near connections, and often far beyond them. If he injures his property, he does harm to those who directly or indirectly derived support from it, and usually diminishes, by a greater or less amount, the general resources of the community. If he deteriorates his bodily or mental faculties, he not only brings evil upon all who depended on him for any portion of their happiness, but disqualifies himself for rendering the services which he owes his fellow-creatures....[3]

Mill's initial response to this view is as follows:

> I fully admit that the mischief which a person does to himself may seriously affect, both through their sympathies and their interests, those nearly connected with him and, in a

[1] *On Liberty*, p. 195.
[2] *Ibid.*, p. 194.
[3] *Ibid.*, p. 210-11.

minor degree, society at large. When, by conduct of this sort, *a person is led to violate a distinct and assignable obligation to any other person or persons*, the case is taken out of the self-regarding class....[1]

He gives some examples. He says that if a man "through intemperance or extravagance, becomes unable to pay his debts" or if a man with children "becomes from the same cause incapable of supporting or educating them," he can "justly be punished." Thus, "no person ought to be punished simply for being drunk; but a soldier or a policeman should be punished for being drunk on duty."[2] This seems reasonably clear, except that Mill has not made it clear whether failing to satisfy an obligation one has to a particular person, or persons, is a *necessary* or *sufficient* condition[3] for harming that person, or persons.

Mill, then, goes immediately on to say something which appears to be very different, despite the inappropriate use of "in short":

> Whenever, in short, *there is a definite damage, or a definite risk of damage, either to an individual or to the public*, the case is taken out of the province of liberty, and placed in that of morality or law.[4]

Perhaps this is a further condition for harming someone else/others. Mill may be saying that in order to harm another/others, *two* conditions must be satisfied: (1) One must be under an obligation to that person, or persons, *and* (2) one must cause a definite damage, or definite risk of damage, to that person, or persons. Or Mill might be giving us a second way that we can harm others. In this case, Mill would be saying that you can be said to harm another/others if: (1) You fail to satisfy a particular obligation you have to another/others *or* (2) you cause a definite damage, or definite risk of damage to another/others. The second interpretation seems consistent with what he says next:

> But with regard to the merely contingent, or, as it may be called, constructive injury which a person causes to society,

---

[1] *On Liberty*, p. 212. Italics are mine.

[2] *Ibid.*, p. 213.

[3] If X is a necessary condition for Y, then "If Y, then X" is true. If X is a sufficient condition for Y, then "If X, then Y" is true.

[4] *On Liberty*, p. 213. Italics are mine.

by *conduct which neither violates any specific duty to the public, nor occasions perceptible hurt to any assignable individual except himself,* the inconvenience is one which society can afford to bear, for the sake of the greater good of human freedom.[1]

To further complicate things, there was a passage in the introduction to *On Liberty* which is relevant to this topic:

> There are also many positive acts for the benefit of others, which he may rightfully be compelled to perform; such as to give evidence in a court of justice; to bear his fair share in the common defence, or in any other joint work necessary to the interest of the society of which he enjoys the protection; and to perform certain acts of individual beneficence, such as saving a fellow-creature's life, or interposing to protect the defenceless against ill-usage, things which whenever it is obviously a man's duty to do, he may rightfully be made responsible to society for not doing. A person may cause evil to others not only by his actions but by his inaction, and in either case he is justly accountable to them for the injury.[2]

Is this yet a third way that we can harm another/others, or can what he says here be subsumed under the other two?

In any case, there are too many vague phrases in what Mill has said about when we have caused harm to others: e.g., "definite damage," "definite risk of damage," and "perceptible hurt." Depending on how these phrases are understood, we might be greatly, or very little, restricted in our behavior when we follow Mill's principle that we should be able to act as we please as long as we don't harm others. If I offend someone through my behavior, as can easily happen, have I caused a "definite damage" to that other person? It seems clear from the general spirit of *On Liberty*, that Mill would say "no."

Some have pointed out that, to defend the position Mill seems to advocating, we need to make at least two crucial distinctions: (1) We must distinguish between *harm* and *offense*. "Harm" should not include instances of someone's behavior violating another person's moral code, which would properly be called "offense" instead. (2) We must

---

[1] *On Liberty*, p. 213. Italics are mine.
[2] *Ibid.*, p. 137.

distinguish between *harm* and *setting a bad example*. When one "sets a bad example" the negative effects are "mediated by the free and informed consent of the individuals affected,"[1] which would not be true of a genuine case of harm.

One last important point. Although Mill would not permit society to forcibly prevent an individual from performing distasteful actions which do not clearly harm others, he does point out that other citizens have the right, and sometimes even an ethical duty, to try to influence the person to change his behavior. Mill is marking out the boundary between the area where the *State* is entitled to forbid actions by individuals and where it is not. It should be remembered, however, that the "moral universe can[not] solely be encompassed by the relationship between the individual and the state."[2] Mill does not say that all the actions which the State must permit are morally praiseworthy actions. Even though the *State* may not interfere — there should not be compulsion or punishment for actions which don't harm others — there will certainly be occasions when other individuals, as individuals, rather than representatives of the State, may be justified in trying to *influence* a person's behavior.

> [A person] cannot rightfully be compelled to do or forbear because it will be better for him to do so, because it will make him happier, because, in the opinions of others, to do so would be wise, or even right. These are good reasons for remonstrating with him, or reasoning with him, or persuading him, or entreating him, but not for compelling him, or visiting him with any evil in case he do otherwise.[3]

The last chapter of *On Liberty* is concerned with "Applications" of Mill's principle. In the first application, Mill makes it clear that he doesn't intend his principle to rule out competitions and free trade, because the losers claim that they have been harmed: "society admits no right, either legal or moral, in the disappointed competitors to immunity from this kind of suffering." He maintains that the State may

[1] See Pyle, *Op. Cit.*, p. xvi, for a discussion of these two distinctions.
[2] Daniel Callahan, "Minimalist Ethics: On the Pacification of Morality," in Francis J. Beckwith, *Do the Right Thing, A Philosophical Dialogue on the Moral Issues of Our Time*, Jones & Bartlett, Sudbury, Mass., 1996, p. 57.
[3] *On Liberty*, p. 135.

interfere "only when means of success have been employed which it is contrary to the general interest to permit — namely, fraud or treachery, and force."[1]

Mill would also permit the sale of dangerous products, such as poisons; but he allows the State to provide warnings and ask for the intended use, to try to limit at least cases of unintended harm occurring. In another application, Mill says that adults should be allowed to spend their money as they wish, even on products like alcohol which may cause them harm:

> Their choice of pleasures, and their mode of expending their income, after satisfying their legal and moral obligations to the State and to individuals, are their own concern, and must rest with their own judgment.[2]

But Mill would allow the heavier taxation of a product such as alcohol as long as the reason given for it is that the State must raise money somehow and, the product not being a necessity for life, it is better to raise money this way than through a means which would take more away from those just getting by. Taxation should not be used to "discourage conduct which it deems contrary to the best interests of the agent," which would be inconsistent with Mill's principle that the State should not be limiting citizens' freedom for their own good.

In the most questionable application, Mill considers whether people should be permitted to sell themselves into slavery.[3] Many think that Mill's position on this issue is not consistent with the rest of *On Liberty*:

> The reason for not interfering, unless for the sake of others, with a person's voluntary acts, is consideration for his liberty. His voluntary choice is evidence that what he so chooses is desirable, or at least endurable, to him, and his good is on the whole best provided for by allowing him to take his own means of pursuing it. But by selling himself for a slave, he abdicates his liberty; he forgoes any future use of it beyond that single act. He therefore defeats, in his own case, the very

---

[1] *On Liberty*, p. 227.

[2] *Ibid.*, pp. 233-4.

[3] Some have claimed that Mill had the institution of marriage in mind when he discussed selling oneself into slavery. See Pyle, *Op. Cit.*, p. x.

purpose which is the justification of allowing him to dispose of himself. He is no longer free....The principle of freedom cannot require that he should be free not to be free.[1]

Is this seemingly paternalistic position consistent with the general principle of *On Liberty*? How can Mill maintain that the State should never interfere with a person's liberty of action just for his own good, but only when he is about to harm others, and yet also say that a person should not be permitted to sell himself into slavery, which would seem to only harm the person himself?

I can see how an individualist might have problems with Mill's forbidding a person to sell himself into slavery — even if it is on the grounds of trying to protect his freedom — because it is restricting the person's liberty to act, when he is not endangering others. Mill seems to be placing more value on *liberty in the abstract* than on the particular individual's desires. Freedom is crucial to individualists, but it is important only so that particular individuals can act on *their own* desires, rather than on others' desires. Mill seems to be telling the individual who wants to sell himself into slavery that he can't desire that, it's not proper, which would bother an individualist.

But Mill isn't an individualist. He is only a supporter of individualist policies as a means to the collective good. And he is looking to the future, rather than restricting himself to what presently existing people happen to want. Freedom, as a general policy, is necessary for the development of a better society for Mill, even if presently existing people don't want it!

Mill's views on education — a subject of continuing interest to him, since through proper education there is hope for the future — are presented as his next "application." Mill believes that the State should enforce education, but not "tak[e] upon itself to direct that education:"

> An education established and controlled by the State should only exist, if it exist at all, as one among many competing experiments, carried on for the purpose of example and stimulus, to keep the others up to a certain standard of excellence.[2]

---

[1] *On Liberty*, p. 236.
[2] *Ibid.*, p. 240.

What does Mill have against the State taking control of all education? Again he is concerned about "the tyranny of the majority:" "A general State education is a mere contrivance for molding people to be exactly like one another."[1]

Mill does think that the State should administer "public examinations," starting at an early age, "so as to make the universal acquisition, and what is more, retention, of a certain minimum of general knowledge virtually compulsory."[2] This will ensure that all citizens are educated, which is necessary to bring about a better society. But Mill adds two qualifications to his view that the State should administer these examinations: (1) "The examinations...in the higher branches of knowledge should...be entirely voluntary," so the State won't have the power "to exclude any one from professions," and (2) "the knowledge required for passing an examination...should, even in the higher classes of examinations, be confined to facts and positive science exclusively."

Mill ends *On Liberty* by giving three reasons why it is best to keep government interference in our lives to a minimum: (1) It is generally the case that "the thing to be done is likely to be better done by individuals than by the government." (2) "Government operations tend to be everywhere alike," rather than allowing for experimentation which may lead to improvements. Finally, (3) Mill is concerned about "the great evil of adding unnecessarily to [government's] power." Adding to the government's power is not an evil *per se*, for Mill, but an evil because of its consequences:

> Every function superadded to those already exercised by the government causes its influence over hopes and fears to be more widely diffused, and converts, more and more, the active and ambitious part of the public into hangers-on of the government, or of some party which aims at becoming the government....[T]he absorption of all the principal ability of the country into the governing body is fatal, sooner or later, to the mental activity and progressiveness of the body itself.[3]

This last passage echoes the position Mill has adopted from the opening pages of *On Liberty* to the end, that the guiding principle in

---

[1] *On Liberty*, p. 239.

[2] *Ibid.*, p. 240.

[3] *Ibid.*, pp.244-7.

social or political philosophy should be the principle of utility, where utility is understood to be "grounded in the permanent interests of man as a progressive being."

Study Questions

1. What is the main principle which Mill wishes to defend in *On Liberty*? On what basis does he say that he will defend it?

2. How can Mill be a hedonistic utilitarian — a view which advocates "the greatest happiness of the greatest number" — and yet also be concerned about "the tyranny of the majority"?

3. Summarize and evaluate Mill's argument that people should be permitted to express any opinion they wish (to an adult audience)?

4. How does Mill argue for the State's permitting expressions of individuality — which includes people being allowed to live their lives as they please — as long as *others* are not harmed in the process? Are you convinced by what he has to say?

5. Has Mill made it clear when we can be said to have harmed others? Can you think of how Mill could have more clearly distinguished between genuinely harming others and in lesser ways negatively affecting them?

6. How do you think Mill would feel about gun control legislation? Why?

7. Why does Mill believe that people should not be permitted to sell themselves into slavery? Does his view make sense?

8. Do you find Mill's concerns about public education and his general position that government involvement in our lives should be kept to a minimum to be consistent with his overall utilitarian view?

5

Final Assessment

We are now in a position to draw some conclusions about Mill's view of how individuals and the State should, and should not, act. In particular, we want to ask: (a) whether Mill has a view which is consistent and, if so, (b) whether it is defensible, and (c) whether he has found a solution to the long-standing debate between Individualism and Collectivism. Let us consider each issue in turn.

I have argued that Mill is consistently a utilitarian[1], which is a collectivist philosophy. Mill believes that both individuals and the State have an ethical obligation to perform those actions which are likely to result in the greatest net good consequences, or the least bad consequences, taking everyone into account. As a *hedonistic* utilitarian, Mill believes that it is the pleasure or happiness that is likely to result which should be considered as good consequences, and the displeasure or unhappiness that is likely to result which should be considered as bad consequences. Furthermore, since Mill believes that not all pleasures are qualitatively the same, the *kinds* of pleasure, as well as the quantity, must be taken into account in deciding which action is right.

What is really crucial for Mill is that we not limit our calculations to the effects on currently existing human beings, if actions which are

---

[1] More specifically, an *act* utilitarian.

performed now can affect future human beings as well. Whereas the actions of ordinary human beings are unlikely to affect other than a few currently existing human beings, this is not true of the actions of the State. Current government policies can affect future generations. It is important, then, to look to the future to see which policies are likely to lead *in the long run* to the best consequences. Mill believes in the possibility of *progress*.[1] The right policies now can lead to more human beings enjoying more pleasurable lives, both in terms of the quantity and quality of pleasure, in the future.

The policies Mill has in mind, as being the right ones to bring about a better society, are policies generally advocated by individualists. Mill does not advocate these policies *for their own sake*, as an individualist would, but only as a *means* to the collective good. This is why Mill should be consistently classified as a collectivist, even when he is most ardently defending individual rights in *On Liberty*. The very idea of "individual rights," for Mill, rests on utilitarian grounds. (See Chapter Five of *Utilitarianism*.)

Mill believes that the *general policy* of protecting individual rights — to express opinions, to lead one's life according to one's own values as long as one doesn't harm others in the process, and to combine with others for any purpose other than harming others — is likely to lead to humanity's prospering. It will allow the truth to emerge and be fully understood, and provide the proper conditions for genius, and creativity in general, to flourish. In addition to the benefits humanity derives from the truth and creativity, each human being will be happier being allowed to express his or her own individuality, and "where there is more [happiness] in the units there is more in the mass which is composed of them."

Mill recognizes that the majority of people may not appreciate the long-term benefits of permitting individual expression. They may find many instances of individual expression to be offensive and/or self-destructive. But, unless the behavior is clearly harming *others*, others should not be permitted to *force* the individuals to change their behavior. Mill says that we must guard against "the tyranny of the majority," who aren't necessarily thinking of what general policies serve "the permanent interests of man as a progressive being." Again, for Mill, the *general policy* of permitting individual expression and lifestyles, as long as others are not clearly harmed, is more beneficial to

---

[1] According to Andrew Pyle, "*progress* is Mill's creed." (Pyle, *Op. Cit.*, p. xvii.)

humanity than not permitting it, even though this may not be true of some *particular* expressions of individuality. A potential genius who destroys her own talent may be a loss to the world, but better that than to create a climate which produces no geniuses at all. Mill would argue that a person who is aware that the potential genius is destroying her talent may be obligated to try to *influence* her to change her behavior, but cannot *force* her to do so.

Mill's overall position does seem to be consistent, but there may be problems with some of the details. Some have expressed concerns about his distinctions between higher and lower pleasures and actions which harm others versus those which others may object to, but don't really cause them harm. Even if there should be problems with these distinctions, it would not affect the consistency of Mill's general position. They are just details to work out in order to practically apply his view. This may seem less obviously true about the distinction between harming and not harming others, because we need to know what counts as harming others in order to understand the central thesis of *On Liberty*: "the only purpose for which power can be rightfully exercised over any member of a civilised community, against his will, is to prevent harm to others." But the central thesis of *On Liberty* is not the central thesis of Mill's overall philosophy. The central thesis of Mill's overall philosophy is the acceptance of Utilitarianism: "I regard utility as the ultimate appeal on all ethical questions...." In *On Liberty,* Mill is only concerned with how the State, in the amount of power it exercises over its citizens, can best achieve the goal of Utilitarianism. So, even though the distinction between harming others versus not harming others is crucial to *On Liberty*, it is but a detail in the practical application of the central thesis of Mill's overall philosophy. I would, therefore, suggest that Mill's view is essentially consistent and, assuming it is defensible, then some work needs to be done on the details.

But is Mill's position defensible? Mill clearly accepts the following views which others might question: (a) Collectivism, rather than Individualism, is the correct view of the ultimate goal of human life. (b) The principle of Utilitarianism is the most defensible collectivist theory. (c) Through education and the right social policies, we can achieve a better society than the one which presently exists.[1] (d) A better society would be one in which more citizens enjoy the higher pleasures in life and identify their own happiness with the good of all.

---

[1] Or, at least, than the society which existed in Mill's day.

(e) The State's adopting general policies associated with Individualism — giving citizens the right to express their opinions and live their lives as they choose, as long as they don't harm others — is most likely to lead to a better society.

Concerning (a), Mill defends his ultimately collectivist view by maintaining that "every one who receives the protection of society owes a return for the benefit."[1] We are social creatures, we cannot survive on our own; and so we must see ourselves as part of *society*, which then becomes the most important entity. Individualists will question this line of reasoning. Following Hobbes, they may claim that the only reason we consent to live in a society is to protect our individual rights. Society exists to benefit individuals, rather than the other way around. More people seem to accept the philosophy of Collectivism than Individualism, but this doesn't necessarily make it more correct. It is certainly circular to argue that because more people will be happy in a collectivist society than an individualist society, it must be better. Individualists question the very idea that the goal of human life is to make the most number of people happy. Why shouldn't the goal instead be, as Nietzsche would argue, to produce great individuals or great individual achievements? People seem to have fundamentally different intuitions about this issue.

Mill's defense of (b), that Utilitarianism is the most defensible collectivist principle, seems very logical:

> Now, society between human beings, except in the relation of master and slave, is manifestly impossible on any other footing than that the interests of all are to be consulted. Society between equals can only exist on the understanding that the interests of all are to be regarded equally.[2]

Ultimately, though, whether the utilitarian principle equally protects the interests of all depends upon the success of Mill's argument that principles of justice can be defended on utilitarian grounds. I see Chapter Five of *Utilitarianism* as the most critical part of his work. And the most impressive argument in that chapter, based on an insight derived from Bentham, is that if the idea of justice doesn't rest on an objective principle, such as what serves utility, we're in trouble. It is too dangerous to leave principles of justice up to people's intuition.

---

[1] *On Liberty*, Chapter Four, p. 205.
[2] *Utilitarianism*, Chapter Three, p. 285.

As for (c), Mill is certainly optimistic in believing that we can bring about a better society. Mill's optimism rests in large part on his belief that it is nurture, rather than nature, which largely determines the behavior of human beings. This is certainly a popular view, and Mill believed he had evidence of it in his own case from the general success of, as well as temporary setback from, his unusual upbringing. If he could be molded into becoming a certain type of being, why not others as well?

The discussion of (d) should be separated into (i) whether it is better for human beings to use their higher faculties than not, and (ii) whether it is better for human beings to identify their own happiness with the good of all rather than just what benefits themselves. Mill's belief that it is better for human beings to use their higher faculties rests on his desire to improve the human race, not just make the best of the status quo. It does seem true that human beings who use their higher faculties will be more developed, but will this necessarily make them happier? Mill has stacked the deck in his favor by maintaining that some pleasures are worth more than others. So the least pleasure which one might receive from exercising the higher faculties can, in principle, outweigh much lower-level displeasure: "It is...better to be Socrates dissatisfied than a fool satisfied." Some might question this. Mill's second claim, that it is better for human beings to identify their own happiness with the good of all, rests in part on his acceptance of Collectivism and in part on an empirical thesis that adopting the philosophy of Collectivism is likely to lead to the greatest net happiness for all. Some do believe that if people start thinking and behaving collectivistically that it will lead to more net happiness. Consider, for example, Edward Bellamy's late nineteenth century utopian novel *Looking Backward* where, due to the adoption of collectivistic attitudes, crime is virtually eradicated as well as the inefficiencies of capitalism. Mill's and Bellamy's empirical thesis has, however, been questioned by many others.

Considering theses (a) - (d), I conclude that, although each one can be questioned, none has been shown to be obviously indefensible either. Let us turn now to (e). Mill's utilitarian arguments in defense of the State adopting general policies which are consistent with the philosophy of Individualism are impressive. This leads us to the final issue, which is the main focus of this book. Has Mill found a solution to the long-standing debate between Individualism and Collectivism?

Both the philosophies of extreme Individualism and extreme Collectivism have advantages and disadvantages. Perhaps Mill has found a way to incorporate into his view the advantages of both, while eliminating the disadvantages of each. If so, since it is consistent and at least not obviously indefensible, that would make Mill's view extremely attractive. Unless there is a better way to capture the best of Individualism and Collectivism,[1] Mill may have given us the best view that we can have concerning the relationship between individuals and between the individual and the State. Let us consider what the advantages and disadvantages are of extreme Individualism and extreme Collectivism and then the extent to which Mill has captured the best of each in his theory, while eliminating the disadvantages.

The supporters of extreme Individualism maintain that only if people are maximally free to live their lives as they choose, as long as they allow others to do the same, will talented and hard-working individuals be allowed to reach their full potential and avoid being brought down by potential parasites. In an extreme individualist society, only a minimal government will be needed to settle disputes and ensure that citizens are protected from fraud and force. Government will not be in the business of providing goods and services, which many may not desire, through the forced taxation of citizens. But critics of Individualism maintain that this view is too hard on less fortunate individuals, who need help from others in order to have a chance of a happy life, or even just to survive. They argue that the needy have a right, as human beings, to this aid. Critics, further, claim that the failure of individualists to recognize the connections we have to others prevents them from accepting many shared responsibilities. Finally, in focusing on winning "freedom from the demands of others," what is called *negative liberty*, individualists are accused of taking a way a sense of direction for human beings: "what the ever freer and more autonomous self is free for only grows more obscure."[2] Surely, they argue, "freedom to," called *positive liberty*, should be emphasized, not just "freedom from."

---

[1] It may be possible to develop a position which maintains that Individualism is correct in the overall goal — that we should strive for each individual making the most of his or her potential — and that some collectivist policies can best bring this about. For people to have a chance to fully develop their potential, one could argue, they must be guaranteed adequate heath care, food, shelter and a good education.

[2] R. Bellah, R. Madsen, W. Sullivan, A. Swindler, and S. Tipton, *Habits of the Heart, Individualism and Commitment in American Life*, University of California Press, Berkeley, California, 1985, p. 82.

Extreme collectivists value security and equality more than freedom; when they talk about freedom it is *positive liberty*, rather than *negative liberty*, which is emphasized. Raising the level of the entire society as much as possible is the goal to strive for, rather than allowing some members to prosper, while others are destitute. Instead of the minimal government advocated by individualists, collectivists would like to see government actively involved in raising the level of society by providing many goods and services for its members. But critics of Collectivism point out that to assume that everyone will agree on the values by which society should live is highly unrealistic. At best, agreement might occur among the majority; but why should the majority be entitled to impose its will on those who don't agree? There is no guarantee of rightness in numbers. Individualists will also claim that allowing all the members of society to reap essentially the same rewards, through the redistribution of goods, for unequal contributions is fundamentally unjust.

It seems, to most, as if we have to choose between the philosophies of Individualism and Collectivism and suffer the negative consequences of our choice. Not so, said Mill, who had a vision of what society ought to be in order for humanity to progress, and who was not particularly concerned with fitting his view into the accepted philosophies of Individualism and Collectivism. As Charles Larrabee Street has said, "Mill himself did not think of the problems he was up against" in terms of "the conflict between 'individualism' and 'collectivism'":

> He did not allow his attitude to be determined by "'isms.'".... Mill's real interest was in solving certain problems which presented themselves to him. He cared more about that than he did about the label that his particular solution might wear.[1]

Mill was convinced that we are essentially social creatures, and that we owe each other certain things for the privilege of living in a society and enjoying its benefits. But he also believed that society prospers only if the individuals who make up society are free to express their individuality as long as they do not harm others. We have to choose between the philosophies of Individualism and Collectivism as

---

[1] Charles Larrabee Street, *Individualism and Individuality in the philosophy of John Stuart Mill*, Morehouse Publishing Company, Milwaukee, 1926, p. 5.

Selected Bibliography

Autobiography, John Stuart Mill, The Library of Liberal Arts, New York, 1957.

Collected Works of John Stuart Mill, University of Toronto Press, Toronto, 1989.

On Liberty and Other Essays, John Stuart Mill, edited by John Gray, Oxford University Press, Oxford, 1998. This volume contains: *On Liberty, Utilitarianism, Considerations on Representative Government* and *The Subjection of Women*.

Utilitarianism and Other Writings, edited by Mary Warnock, New American Library, New York, 1974. This volume contains: Mill's "Bentham," *On Liberty* and *Utilitarianism*, as well as Bentham's *Introduction to the Principles of Morals and Legislation* and a lecture of John Austin's.

John Stuart Mill, A Mind at Large, Eugene August, Charles Scribner's Sons, New York, 1975.

John Stuart Mill and Harriet Taylor, F. A. Hayek, Routledge and Kegan Paul, London, 1951.

John Stuart Mill, the Man, Ruth Borchard, Watts Publishing Company, London, 1957.

The English Utilitarians, Leslie Stephen, Peter Smith Publishing Company, New York, 1950.

The Moral Philosophy of John Stuart Mill, Towards Modifications of Contemporary Utilitarianism, Mark Strasser, Longwood Academic Press, Wakefield, New Hampshire, 1991.

Final Assessment

far as what the *overall* goal of human life should be, and Mill has chosen Collectivism. But he feels just as strongly that the best means to achieve the collectivist goal is for the State to adopt many of the policies associated with Individualism. According to Mill, we not only *can* have our cake and eat it too, by combining the best of Collectivism and Individualism, but we *ought* to. It can be argued that Mill's view captures the best of Collectivism in adopting its overall goal, while eliminating the disadvantages people associate with that philosophy with his advocacy of individual liberty in our dealings with others and in government policies. It can also be argued that Mill captures the best of Individualism, by championing individualist general social policies; yet he seems to avoid the concerns that many have with a fully individualistic philosophy, that it doesn't give people something positive to strive for and is likely to pit people against one another instead of having them appreciate their common bond, by insisting that goal of human existence is to bring about a better *society*.

What Mill sought was a "morality grounded on large and wise views of the good of the whole, neither sacrificing the individual to the aggregate nor the aggregate to the individual, but giving to duty on the one hand and to freedom and spontaneity on the other their proper province."[1] Mill, much to his credit, has given us a plausible view which does just that.

Study Questions

1. Do you agree that Mill's overall position seems to be consistent?

2. What concerns do you have about the defensibility of Mill's views?

3. How has Mill attempted to capture the best of the philosophies of Individualism and Collectivism in his views? Do you think he succeeded?

---

1 Mill, *Three Essays on Religion*, quoted in Strasser, *Op. Cit.*, p. 210.